To Pat
Enjoy your
Life Journey

Frank Rutten

Hitting the Road Without a Map...

and other miscalculations

The story of a trip with a goal, but virtually no plan

FRED RUTTER

Willow Moon Publishing

Willow Moon Publishing

Copyright © 2019 by Fred Rutter. Published by Willow Moon Publishing Lancaster, PA 17601 willow-moon-publishing.com
All rights reserved. No part of this publication may be reproduced or transmitted in any form or by many means except for brief quotations in printed reviews, without the prior permission of the publisher.
Cataloging Data Rutter, Fred
Hitting the Road Without a Map and other miscalculations – an RV Trip West –1st U.S. Edition Summary: The story of a trip with a goal - but virtually no plan. A travel memoir and a photo essay of a journey from Ohio to Oregon As well as a personal meditation on the nature of relationships, facing fears, and becoming mindful of living in the moment.287 pages; 152 x 229 mm.
Paperback ISBN: 978-1-948256-40-7. 1) Memoir – travel & pictorial. 2) Memoir-RV Travel / American West highways. 3) Travel American west – Description, present day.3) Sobriety / recovery – sober living. 4) Travel photography – American West, present day.5) National Parks travel – Badlands – Mount Rushmore-Yellowstone.6) Travel-Ohio to Oregon. I. Hitting the Road Without a Map and other miscalculations – an RV Trip West. II. Rutter, Fred.
Printed in the United States on acid free paper. Edited by Cayn Pine. Typeset: Palatino. Design by Jodi Stapler

While the author has made every effort to provide accurate telephone numbers and Internet addresses at the time of publication, neither the publisher nor the author assumes any responsibility for errors, or for changes that occur after publication. Further, the publisher does not have any control over and does not assume responsibility for author or third-party Web sites or their content, and neither does this author. Inclusion is for informational purposes only. No part of this book may be used or reproduced in any manner whatsoever without written permission except in the case of brief quotations embodied in critical articles and reviews. For information, contact the author through Turkey Rock LLC, P. O. Box 193, Lithopolis, Ohio 43136-0193

Dedication

Normal convention dictates choosing one. Being an alcoholic, with an addictive personality, I choose more.

To Tammy, for putting up with me and for encouraging me to write, even though I cause you aggravation

To Todd, Amy, and my good friend Tom

To all those who are recovering in alcohol and substance abuse programs—your new life is to be enjoyed

For those wondering if it might be time to give sobriety a try—it is, right now

And to fellow travelers everywhere—pay attention to it all, and enjoy

Table of Contents

Preface		8
Introduction		10
1	*Genesis – from the beginning*	14
2	*The RV needs to go to Oregon, now – with some slight delays*	22
3	*Are you ready to go yet?*	30
4	*The Trip*	37
5	*Badlands*	55
6	*Repairs*	76
7	*Wind*	98
8	*Yellowstone*	127
9	*Free Range*	159
10	*The Pacific*	190
11	*Oregon Rain*	222
12	*The Real World*	237
13	*Separation*	252
14	*Homeward Bound*	264
15	*Aftermath – Renewed Faith*	274
Epilogue		276
References		279
Acknowledgments		281
Special Acknowledgments		285
About the Author		286

Drive 3,014 miles

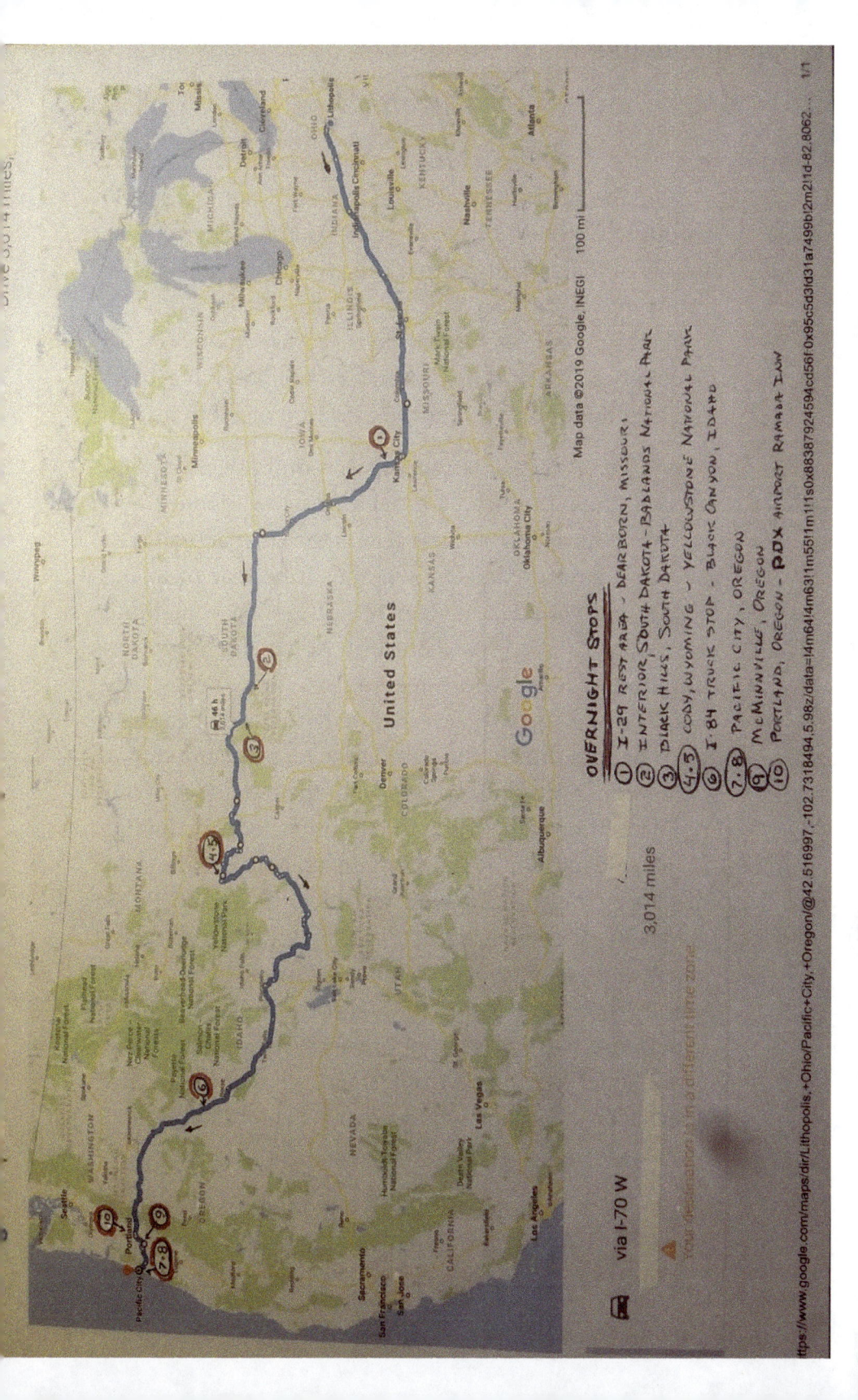

via I-70 W

3,014 miles

Your destination is in a different time zone

OVERNIGHT STOPS
1. I-29 REST AREA - DEARBORN, MISSOURI
2. INTERIOR, SOUTH DAKOTA - BADLANDS NATIONAL PARK
3. BLACK HILLS, SOUTH DAKOTA
4, 5. CODY, WYOMING - YELLOWSTONE NATIONAL PARK
6. I-84 TRUCK STOP - BLACK CANYON, IDAHO
7, 8. PACIFIC CITY, OREGON
9. McMINNVILLE, OREGON
10. PORTLAND, OREGON - PDX AIRPORT RAMADA INN

Preface

The actual trip took place from September 30 through October 10, 2018, but so much more was involved than simply embarking, traveling, and finally returning. Because all the people associated with the backstory, and the eventual trip, are members of Alcoholics Anonymous, their last names have been omitted out of respect for the tradition of anonymity.

The AA recovery program emphasizes, among other things, the need for each of us to identify and confront our fears, because fear is the chief activator of all our character defects, whether it be fear of losing something we have, or fear of not getting something we want. I had to confront some of my own unfounded fears before leaving on this journey. My wife Tammy had to wrestle with some of her fears prior to, and during the trip. These fears included that (1) I might not come back, (2) that the dynamics of our relationship might be negatively impacted, and finally (3) a health situation that heightened her personal fear of getting cancer. She was forced to deal with those fears and other ones that cropped up while I was away, alone. My experience of the journey was spiritual and wholly positive in nature. Unfortunately, Tammy's experience was fraught with fear and anxiety, so back to the chief activator of our character defects. At the conclusion, we both had grown emotionally and spiritually, but our paths were vastly different.

To impart a better understanding of the actual adventure, it is necessary to draw the curtain open and illuminate some aspects of life in sobriety, life dealing with mental illness, and living "life on life's terms." These things may be new to some, and they may feel it is not 'in good taste' to be so open about them. However, millions of people deal with these aspects of life all the time—in fact, it is part of their daily experience and should not be separated or ignored. To do so is a disservice and disrespectful of what makes us whole people. Therefore, I talk about these things a lot, for it is who I am today. Including these parts of my life, and those around me, hopefully results in a more complete and honest story.

For readers desiring a true tale of travel and adventure across part of America, in a recreational vehicle (RV), take heart and please proceed, for it is here. The whole story awaits your discovery.

Fred Rutter
Lithopolis, Ohio
March 7, 2019

Introduction

Two guys walk out of a bar, get into a large recreational vehicle (RV) motorhome, which does not belong to them, and head west. The punchline could be the saga that follows, for this is essentially the short version of the story. However, the critical time period between exiting the tavern and entering the vehicle spans several decades. By that time, both men are sober—in fact, they crossed paths in the rooms of alcoholism recovery—and not in a bar—and they really do not know each other all that well. There is a big difference between many brief encounters over the years at AA meetings, and spending a week and a half together in a metal box hurtling down the road. In order to understand how these two guys, basically cordial acquaintances, ended up heading across the country in someone else's motorhome, it is necessary to go back and review some of the "begats" or the true origins.

The critical stepping off point for all the participants in this saga began with them getting sober. That is where a new life began for all of them. Active participation in a program of recovery, Alcoholics Anonymous, is how they all met. There was a time way back in their past when the two intrepid travelers may well have walked out of a bar and commenced upon an unscripted journey, with or without the permission of the RV owner. Those adventures, fueled by the inhibition lowering properties of alcohol and mind-altering substances, plus the character defects of selfishness and self-centeredness, typically ended in shame and remorse, or in the worst cases, tragically. That is no longer the sort of life either one of them lives today.

A bit of old wisdom states, *"it is not the destination, but the journey"* that is important. True enough, provided the person is actually paying attention. Another, states something to the effect of, *"the hardest part of any journey is getting through the back gate."* Both sayings are apropos to this author, especially as they relate to the trip undertaken in the following story. So-called sayings of wisdom spring from the immense well of human knowledge, whether one cares to give them their proper due respect or not. Greater understanding, or a sense of awe and awareness, may come suddenly, while other more sublime transformations take a bit of time, or pain, before the realization of a change in perspective solidifies. Several aspects of a personal transformation played out in my life leading up to, during, and after the journey.

Another, equally critical aspect of this particular saga is one of opportunity. Break the bonds of convention! Hit the road! Two Siren calls percolating below the constraints of everyday busyness and fast-paced living in all of us. We tell ourselves we will do just that—someday. But when the opportunity arises, do we recognize it, and do we run with it? Life, responsibility, and guilt often hold us back. The reasons are always logical and justifiable, and yet we are left with a gnawing sense of regret for having not acted upon the chance. So, what happens when we actually do it? The experiences will be different for each individual because circumstances and the emotional baggage we carry will be unique and alter our perspective to what unfolds. Much depends upon one's attitude.

What originated as a straightforward trip became much more than that for me, and possibly for others along the way. More often than not, we are unaware of the effects we have on others. That is their story to tell, from their own perspective. This is a description of one specific part of a much larger life journey—a single important chapter, if you will, of my life.

The bits and pieces for this adventure began aligning years before the RV ever left the parking lot. Of course, none of us could even imagine or know it at the time. Part of the wonder of life is that it can be appreciated further, upon reflection, on what has transpired over time. For many, the appreciation and wonder is not given a second thought, either when the events are occurring, or afterward. I find that sad, for they miss much joy and self-discovery. Throughout my life, I have endeavored to be conscious of life as it unfolds in the moment. The term *du jour* is "mindfulness." However, in order to put the present in better perspective, it is necessary to look at the past, which is the case in this particular tale that was supposed to be a simple trip from Point A to Point B.

Many trips are meticulously planned down to the finest detail, with the expectation that the planning is what will make it great and problem-free. The trip recounted in this story was the total opposite of that. Circumstances prevented it from being meticulously planned because no one was even sure if it would happen, or when. The only knowns were where it would start and the final destination, providing it was necessary to do at all. It was a delivery trip of an RV, pure and simple. All other factors would be influenced by whether the vehicle still required moving, the timing, and the people actually undertaking the task.

Once the wheels actually began rolling, a series of miscalculations and unforeseen events prompted new decisions, and a new outlook, by the two guys who ended up with this errand. Instead of fighting these situations and trying to force a regimented plan into place, they chose to embrace the challenges and view them as opportunities to be entirely free out on the road. That attitude allowed them to truly let go, and be transformed by the whole experience.

Chapter 1
Genesis – from the beginning

Somehow, I found myself agreeing to take a trip across the country with four days' notice, while my chagrined wife listened to the phone conversation from across the kitchen table. An undertaking like this did not materialize completely out of thin air.

It certainly was not the intent of the participants in this trip to slowly assemble over a period of more than twenty years. In fact, their coming together was not a conscious act at all. Individually, their primary objective was to not screw their lives up any more than they already had and to try to repair the damage done by a former way of living which no longer worked. They accomplished this by getting sober and working the program of Alcoholics Anonymous. Saved from the abyss, the new goal was to pass the message of hope to others who found themselves at a similar crossroads in their lives. A person can meet a number of interesting people this way.

I first met Todd in the late 1980s or early 1990, at an Alcoholics Anonymous meeting in Groveport, Ohio. Fairly new to the program, and a bit dazed and confused as we all are when newly sober, he had an air of self-assuredness and ego-driven control that I found off-putting, so I kept some distance. I had about five years sobriety by then and wrongly assumed that I had a rather good grasp on life. Todd managed to fall in with a crowd that felt they ought to write a much better, and shorter version of the "AA Big Book," that would be easier for all to follow, and would provide a rapid path to sobriety, just like in 'the old days.' In AA, this is tantamount to blasphemy, so I observed this group with measured skepticism. As it says in "The Big Book," the AA slang for the book _Alcoholics Anonymous_, John Barleycorn is the great disciplinarian of those who defy the simple recovery tools presented to us. One either embraces the whole program or dies drunk—or just as bad, struggles on in a declining state of miserable existence. As the years went by, some of the participants of this zealotry did in fact crash and burn, and others simply lost some of their reformation zeal and moved on. Todd did not succumb to the siren call of a fast fix, stayed sober, and grew emotionally and spiritually. He went through a messy divorce, got into a new relationship with an attractive girl named Michelle, and gradually disappeared from my orbit. Eventually, he moved one county south, to Circleville, Ohio in Pickaway County.

Late in the 1980s, I met a woman at one of my regular meetings. Over the next three years it evolved into a classic case of "boy meets girl on AA campus," and Tammy and I were married in 1991. Our nuptial bliss soon became buffeted by bouts of depression, and other behaviors, which we believed could be solved by love and diligently working the 12 Step recovery program. Eight years later, Tammy was diagnosed as being bipolar (manic depression). Thus, commenced a multi-year ordeal of finding the correct medications, psychologists, and counselors, to help her manage her condition. Meanwhile, my own mental and physical condition deteriorated under the stress, so I reached out for help, at Tammy's behest, and took a twelve-week course from NAMI (the National Association of Mental Illness) to understand her condition better, and how to improve mine. Our work together to live life on life's terms continues, just like the work on sobriety—on a daily basis. Our life is not all smooth sailing, nor is it all grim either, for we are truly best friends, and rely on each other's love and support, plus our shared interests in active participation in recovery, history, antiques, collecting, music, and travel.

During the ensuing years, I was working long hours while rising through the ranks at Mid-Ohio Foodbank, and had changed the AA meetings I attended to accommodate that. Todd and I were cordial to each other on the rare occasions our paths crossed, but that was about it. We were living our own lives.

Around 1993, a new AA meeting started on Saturday night down in the Hocking Hills of Southeastern Ohio, in a small Hocking County hamlet called South Perry. I knew Steve, the guy who started the South Perry meeting, because he had attended the

Asbury 12 & 12 AA meeting in Groveport, but he wanted to have a meeting closer to where he lived in Hocking County. Ironically, the Asbury meeting is where Tammy and I first met and was one of three AA meetings in Groveport at that time. Unfortunately, Steve did not stay sober, but the meeting he started lives on.

The word in the area AA meeting rooms was that the meeting down in South Perry was a good one, although it was definitely down in the middle of nowhere. South Perry, and the Hocking Hills, are in Appalachian foothills. As a result, Tammy and I had never attended. Why go that far when there were several meetings only five miles down the road? Over time, the Groveport Saturday night meeting disintegrated as remnants of the old "make AA great again" clan took over. I hung in there for another year or so but was getting more of a resentment from each Saturday night meeting than I was enhancing my sobriety.

November 5, 2005, we bought Tammy her dream car, a used 2000 Ford Escort ZX2 sports car, from Tansky Used AutoMart in Lancaster, Ohio. For the initial drive, after signing all the paperwork and paying for the car with our MasterCard, we decided to head down to South Perry and attend that AA meeting for the first time. The curvy roads and hills would make for a fine test drive. At that meeting, we met Tom and Amy. We quickly became good friends, and over the years we visited them at their hilltop home in Vinton County, even deeper into Appalachia. We also enjoyed lots of conversations with them before and after meetings, and over meals. I began to attend the

South Perry meeting on a regular basis. Todd would show up there periodically with Michelle, but later she disappeared into a fog of her own creation, which happens when one resumes using alcohol and other substances. Then Todd sort of faded away as well, but eventually reappeared with a new girlfriend named Margy. She was an "earth person," which in AA slang means she did not share our problem with drinking, and other substances. Margy reduced the chaos in Todd's life immensely.

Fast forward ten years: Amy retired from her job at Adena Health in Chillicothe, Ohio, and Tom retired from his job as an independent over-the-road semi-tractor trailer driver. They decided to buy a recreational vehicle, also known as an RV, or motor home, and travel around the country. Their first trip was to New England. They got sideswiped, in Vermont, by an out-of-control dump truck pulling a backhoe on a trailer. The RV was totaled in the wreck, but that did not dampen their wanderlust, so they bought another RV. This one was a little nicer, and a little bigger. The idea now was to explore the feasibility of eventually living and traveling in an RV fulltime and leave the Vinton County hilltop in Southeast Ohio for good.

The test was a success, in that they enjoyed the life, and had figured out the logistics necessary for being out on the road with no permanent address. So they traded in that unit in for an even larger and better RV—a 37 foot long 2007 Southwind motorhome with a Ford V-10 gasoline engine, three slide-out room extensions, a bathroom with a shower, a washer/dryer, full-size stove and refrigerator, a microwave, multiple TVs, carpeting, as well as a leather couch/hide-away bed in the combined living room/dining room/kitchen area. It was literally a house on wheels and would fit the bill for fulltime living on the road. They took a several month-long trip to Florida and Mississippi to get used to their prospective new home, but Tom was not feeling well and they returned home a bit early. It turned out he had lung cancer. Tom died six months later during the summer of 2017. We were all bummed out. Amy lost her husband and partner, AA lost a valued member, and I lost one of my very best friends.

Amy knew she had to move on in life. At first, that meant trying to proceed with the nomad life without Tom. She decided to take a winter trip to the southwest in the RV with one of her sisters. The shakedown cruise for them would be a late October weekend camping trip to Rocky Fork State Park, near Hillsboro in southern Ohio. Amy asked me to help her learn how to drive the beast. For years I had driven big straight trucks for Mid-Ohio Foodbank, first as a driver, then as the transportation and fleet manager. One of my duties was truck driver training. I had retired the first week of October 2017 and was looking for things to do, and this was a way to help a friend. Tom had done all the driving on their previous trips, so the handling of a very big vehicle would be a new experience for Amy. I gave her pointers and strategies for making turns at intersections, etc., but thought to myself that this motorhome was way different than a truck. The lines of sight seemed different, and I was not sure how it maneuvered or handled, and it felt rather 'mushy' on the road and going around corners.

Amy was doing the driving. I was there to provide instruction and moral support where needed. She did great.

The state park trip went well, so next up was their trip out west for a couple of months. Amy shared photos on Facebook of a glass orb containing some of Tom's ashes, positioned in various places along the way so he could appreciate the journey as well. She visited a former college classmate named Lindsay in San Diego, and it turned out they still hit it off after all the intervening years. Lindsay was contemplating a move to Oregon and asked Amy if she would consider joining her. The proposal had appeal, and logic as well. The house on the hill in Vinton County was more than one person could deal with. Just maintaining the vertigo-inducing driveway was enough of a worry, and besides, she and Tom had planned to sell the house and live on the road in the RV together. That plan had lost its luster, with Tom now gone.

Amy decided to go for it. They narrowed down the location to the Portland, Oregon area, and a scouting trip to find a house resulted in a single floor rental home in McMinnville, halfway between Portland and Salem, Oregon. AARP magazine rated the town as one of the ten best retirement towns in the country, due to affordability, amenities, walkability, and relative proximity to a lot of natural wonder. The next step was for Amy to sell everything and move, which turned out to be not quite that easy. She told her friends at the South Perry meeting of her plans early in the summer of 2018. The process of selling the house and the RV took a while. In the end, the RV did not sell, and closing on the house sale was delayed multiple times. Meanwhile, Lindsay had moved to their new home in Oregon and was waiting on Amy and the furniture to arrive. It would be a long wait.

Chapter 2
The RV needs to go to Oregon now – with some slight delays

By mid-August, after going through multiple delays with the Vinton County house sale closing, and the apparently dim prospects of unloading the RV anytime soon, Amy determined the best course of action was to proceed with the move to Oregon and have someone else drive the RV out there and she would deal with selling it later. The movers had been retained and scheduled several times, only to be canceled just as often, due to the house sale closing issues. Now she would schedule them again, no matter what, then load up her car and try to beat the moving van to the west coast. Hopefully, the house would finally be sold by then. Todd offered to drive the RV west at a later date.

One Saturday night at the South Perry AA meeting, while standing outside enjoying the warm weather, Amy announced this new plan to everyone, as we had been requesting updates on her sale and move west. I looked at Todd and said, "Well, that sounds like an interesting adventure!"

"Yeah, I thought so too! Wanna go with me?" Todd replied.

"That's a great idea! I would be much more comfortable if he does not do it alone," Amy responded with delight.

"I will be all right, but you're welcome to come," Todd said, looking at us both, but giving me a nod.

"Well, it is settled then! I can check that off my list! What a relief!" exclaimed Amy.

"Not quite done yet," I replied, "I like the sound of it—a road trip across the country, but I do have to talk to Tammy first."

"Of course! Heck, she can come too! I don't care. I just need the thing moved!" Amy exclaimed.

Big John B had been leaning on the stair railing, smoking a cigarette and taking this all in. "Fred, seems like you just 'stepped in it!'" he opined. We all laughed.

The next day I told Tammy the plan. "That sounds like a once in a lifetime adventure! You ought to do it!" she said.

"That's exactly what I thought," I replied, "and you can go too, if you want, but I'm not sure how much fun it would be since we would need to drive at least 500 miles a day in order to make it to Portland in five or six days. It's not going to be a true pleasure trip. In fact, it will probably be a grueling grind most days."

"That, and how would I manage my meds, and what would we do with four cats for over a week?" Years earlier, Tammy had been diagnosed with manic depression, or bipolar disease. It took years to get the medications and the dosages adjusted in order to tamp down the highs and lows and provide some semblance of stability. But there were consequences. The current regimen started at 3 PM with Tegretol. Taken any later than that resulted in a drug hangover the next day. The only problem was that sometimes there was no problem, yet other times the medication would hit her so hard that she would not be able to walk within twenty minutes, and occasionally got toxic and violently ill. The second round of medications, taken at 6 PM often ended with a similar result as the first round. Therefore, her life, and mine to a great extent, had been dictated to by the medication clock. Deviations also had disastrous results. So strict adherence to the medications was the rule. Not taking the medications was worse than the frequent and random side effects of what was supposed to manage her condition.

"You go. I'll stay home and I'll be fine," was Tammy's final pronouncement. I called Amy and told her I was in and asked what the timeline was because I had a commitment the third weekend of September in Marietta, Ohio that I could not change. She assumed the RV move would be completed by mid-September, but it also had to work around any scheduling conflicts Todd might have.

Todd was ready to go within a week, but could not go in mid-October due to a planned vacation with Margy to Hawaii, which was already booked and paid for. He also had a couple of Circleville city council meetings he had to attend. Amy was still waiting to find out when the actual closing would occur on the house and had again scheduled and postponed the movers one more time. The water well failed inspection and had to be re-tested by the county health department, causing a further delay on the closing. Then the buyers ran into some sort of financial glitch. The closing paperwork was not yet ready to be signed by Amy. September was rapidly approaching, and Todd's window of availability was rapidly closing.

Labor Day came and went. Amy was getting aggravated, and Lindsay had been living in their new home in McMinnville, Oregon for over a month and a half now, with virtually no furniture. It was time to do something! She contacted her lawyer and real estate agent to get all her part of the paperwork drawn up and signed. Both advised against this course of action, for there was a risk that things could still go haywire at the closing. "You deal with it!" was her response. Her plan remained the same—schedule the movers again, and have Todd and I drive the RV while she raced across the continent to beat us both. I would be back home in time for the Sons & Daughters of Pioneer Rivermen meeting in Marietta, Ohio. Then Todd informed her that he could not go now because one of his council meetings had a critical vote and he had to attend. Plan foiled!

At the next South Perry meeting, Amy said to me, "Let's you and I drive the RV, and we can tow my Honda. The movers are picking up my stuff this coming week. Because of the delays, Todd might not be available until November, after he gets back from Hawaii."

"That would be a dicey proposition, because of snow out west," I observed.

Up to this point, I had expressed some trepidation to Tammy about my confidence and comfort with the upcoming trip. Prior to retirement, the last several years of my employment at Mid-Ohio Foodbank had been as a transportation analyst, meaning I rarely drove the trucks anymore. I sat at a computer all day long, creating Excel spreadsheets and reports, doing data entry, analyzing data, creating, and doing budget analysis, and serving as the truck fleet maintenance manager. Since retirement, it had now been almost two and a half years since I had spent any considerable time behind the wheel of a large vehicle. This RV certainly qualified as a large vehicle—as big as the trucks I used to drive. However, it was set up more like a bus than a truck, so I figured it would be an entirely new driving experience. Also, even though I had known Todd for over twenty years, I really did not know him—at least not the way one knows a person when they hang out together for hours at a time on a regular basis. Our only exposure to each other had been the hour or so at AA meetings over the years. So, I had no clue, really, what it would be like to be stuck on the road with him for days. I suspected he had some traits, like ultra-conservative politics or a big ego, which I would find intolerable at the worst, or just really irritating at best, if exposed to them for days on end. Just as important, I recognize I have my own habits and foibles that someone else might find irritating, or make fun of, such as being a slow eater, taking a lot of time in the bathroom, or stopping to pee frequently, and that I also love to stop and take pictures all the time. Another factor was entirely fear-based, and that being a fear of harassment or hazing—neither of which I have hardly ever experienced in my life but have always dreaded it anyway. Tammy and I accept these foibles in each other, and respectfully accommodate each other so we are great traveling partners. This upcoming expedition would be all new on several very important fronts—the vehicle and the partner. Nothing about Todd indicated any of these things were probable. There is an acronym used in AA, for the word fear: **F**alse **E**vidence **A**ppearing **R**eal. This was about all my own insecurities playing out in my head. My fear of the unknown was growing and causing me much anxiety. I had shared these escalating misgivings with Tammy over several weeks.

When Amy broached the new arrangement, I said "okay," but I was definitely not okay with it. Arriving home later that evening, I told Tammy the trip was on for next week, but with several major changes. She had been feeding off my growing anxiety and added some of her own, such as fearing there would be an accident, like driving off a cliff or something, and she would lose me forever. Tom and Amy and I had spent a lot of time together over the years, so while this new arrangement was not ideal from an appearance standpoint, I was relatively confident that we probably would not drive each other nuts. Towing a car, well that was a whole new kettle of fish, which made me even more nervous. I have never towed anything, ever, let alone behind a strange vehicle I was already a nervous wreck about driving. I expressed all this to Tammy, and I could tell she was not happy.

The next day, at the Sunday Morning AA meeting in Lancaster, Tammy's sponsor asked how she was doing. "Not well," was her reply, and proceeded to explain.

"Oh, hell no!" Teresa exclaimed. "No man of mine would be driving across the country with another woman, and if he did, he deserves to go over a cliff!"

"You are right!" said Tammy, and that was the end of that! Plan foiled again.

I called Amy when we got home, but she did not answer, so I left a voice message explaining I could not go, and apologized for the bind I just put her in. Not certain she would get the message in time, or wonder where the heck I was, I sent an email detailing what had transpired—my trepidation about driving the RV in general after a couple of years not driving big vehicles, my specific misgivings about towing a car while driving a vehicle I had never driven, and more importantly, my wife's objection to my traveling with another woman no matter who she was.

A day later I received a terse reply, basically stating "all is good." Nevertheless, I felt bad for letting a friend down. From an appearance standpoint, I understood where Tammy was coming from. From my own perspective, I was relieved. A week or so later Amy posted some pictures on Facebook of her sister and her as they headed west.

"Well," I said to Tammy, "that is the end of that. She is on her way west with her sister."

"So why the hell did she not ask her sister in the first place?" was Tammy's angry retort. A few days later, Amy posted a photo of her sister at the wheel, only she was driving the Honda, not the RV. I chose not to inquire about the status of the RV after the frayed nerves I had just caused, and assumed it was all taken care of and I did not need to know. I informed Tammy of what I had observed on Facebook, and my non-response to Amy. Case closed; trip avoided.

Chapter 3
Are you ready to go yet?

On Thursday, September 27, Todd called and talked to Tammy, while I was out in the yard doing something. When I got back in she said, "Call Todd. The RV trip is on, and he is leaving right away."

So I called Todd. "Hey," he said, "are you ready to go yet?"

"Not hardly," I replied. "I had to back out of one of the previous arrangements, so I thought it was all over. Where is the RV anyway?"

"It has been in my driveway for almost two weeks. I've been working on it. Just got the generator working by putting a new fuel pump on it, and a 'jerry can' of gas to run it off of. Also been checking the equipment to make sure we have everything, and that it all works. Just trying to familiarize myself with all this."

"So, when do you want to leave?" I asked.

"I'm ready to go tomorrow, or Saturday at the latest!" Todd replied.

"There is no way I can leave on either of those days! I was not prepared to leave at all, so there are a bunch of things I will have to arrange first. If that does not work out for you, go without me. I will not be offended."

"What do you need to do?"

"Well, for one thing, I don't have a plane ticket, but more importantly, I will have to find someone to open next week's Saturday Men's AA Meeting in Lancaster for me. I'm the secretary. Normally, this would not be much of a problem, but next Saturday we have to meet at another church, and there is one guy who can open that other church because he has the security codes and a key. I usually see him at the Friday Noon Meeting. If he is there, and if he agrees to open the Saturday meeting next week for me, then I can go. If he's not there, or I cannot get a hold of him, then I cannot go. The earliest I can let you know one way or another is tomorrow afternoon. If I can go, how about leaving Monday or Tuesday? I'll have to get a plane ticket, pack, and take care of some other stuff."

"Monday or Tuesday is too late," Todd replied. "I have to get out to Oregon and back on time. Margy and I have a two-week vacation planned to Hawaii. We leave in two weeks. It's already arranged. I have to be back before then."

"Okay," I replied, "I understand. When you get back from your vacation, it will be too close to

November, and bad weather out west. So it's either now, or next spring. I will let you know one way or another on Friday."

"So, you are going to do it?" Tammy asked disgustedly.

"Not for sure yet, but probably," I replied, then sarcastically added, "I can see you're not thrilled."

"No, I'm not! I thought this was all over with! Now it is not! I'm pissed and I'm scared!" Tammy declared, with no ambiguity.

"Wait a minute!" I replied, "I thought the problem was me going out there with Amy and towing a car! Now, it is back to the original plan with just Todd and me, and only driving the RV!"

"Yes, but you've told me how nervous you are driving that thing. You have never driven something like that. I'm afraid something will happen, and you will never come back!" Tammy beseeched.

"I am nervous, but once I drive it, I will probably be fine. I just have to work through my fears. And I'm coming back. I'm not leaving forever!" I responded.

"Go ahead! Do what you want to do! You always do! I'll be fine!" she hissed.

"Thank you. I know you will be fine. This will only be a little over a week," I wanly replied, knowing full well this was not over. The chances this would transpire without a lot more angst was slim to none, at best.

"So, when are you leaving?"

"Looks like it will be Sunday, provided I'm going. I have to see if Lee can open next week's meeting for me. If not, Todd might leave tomorrow," I replied.

Lee was at the AA meeting on Friday, and he was agreeable to opening the men's meeting at the alternate location the following Saturday. I called Todd when I got home.

"Okay, Todd, next week's meeting is covered, and I am on board! What day is your flight back, and what do I need to bring?"

"I am booked on American Airlines to come back on October 10. I can put you on my flight if there are any seats left. Bring whatever snacks and food you want to eat, and a comforter or something to sleep in," he said.

"I already checked Southwest Airlines. Why the food and sleeping stuff? You're not planning to eat at restaurants along the road and staying in motels?"

"Oh, sure, we could buy some meals, but I was figuring staying in the RV and fixing our own meals, even though Amy had cleaned it in order to sell it. It will be cheaper that way.

"Okay, I can definitely go with cheap! I just wanted to find out what your strategy was, and I am fine with that. I will bring stuff like peanut butter & jelly, cereal, and fruit. By the way, is there a road atlas in the RV? I already checked a logical route on Google, and it looks like this will take a least five and a half days, providing we make at least five hundred miles a day. It is about 2,700 miles from Columbus to Portland, and McMinnville is another 40 or so miles."

"Yeah, that's about what I figured too," Todd replied. "But I was hoping to see some stuff along the way, if you are all right with that. Let us not kill ourselves getting out there! We have time. I'll check for a road atlas in the RV. Really was not looking for one while I was fixing all this other stuff and filling the water tank. Got it fueled up this morning. This thing was pretty well cleaned out by Amy when she was trying to sell it, and I have spent the past week, and a couple hundred bucks, getting it ready!"

"Well, I am all for seeing stuff!" I replied. "When I was looking at the map, it looked like there were a lot of parks and scenic stuff, especially in Idaho and Oregon that would be right along the route. And thank you in advance for getting this beast ready!"

I compared the cost of American Airlines and Southwest. The difference was minimal, and the Southwest cost had gone up a bit just since yesterday. The main difference was the route. Southwest went Portland to Chicago to Columbus, whereas American went Portland to Los Angeles to Columbus. That was a lot of flying time, plus a layover at LAX, so I booked the flight on Southwest.

Next, I went to Walgreens and bought all the photographic film they had, and then went to the bank to get money for Tammy, and money for me. By this time, Tammy was silent and depressed. She did request that we do a test drive to the airport together on Saturday if I expected her to pick me up when I returned. This we did, and also picked up supplies at Walmart on our way home. Saturday evening, I finished packing. I was as ready as I could be. Tammy, however, still had great trepidation about this, but was being stoic and putting on a "game face." I tried to assure her it would all be fine, but she responded that I could not make that kind of guarantee, and now it sounded like Todd and I were going to embark on a fun trip, like *Pee Wee's Big Adventure* instead of a straight forward transportation trip. The conversation concluded with Tammy declaring, "You are going off and having fun without me!"

I knew she was dealing with fear—fear that something would happen to me, fear about being alone for a long period of time, and fear that I might find a new running buddy. For Tammy, fear gets translated as being scared, and she often deals with being scared with anger, for lashing out in anger gives the illusion of power and being in control of the situation. We had been through this on other occasions, like my numerous business trips to Chicago over the years. But this type of reaction had gotten better over time as a result of counseling, reading, and Tammy's extensive personal analysis and self-searching over the years. My job is to try not to react personally, and to accept whatever reaction she exhibits by accepting that something is unacceptable, and let it go. There was a high probability that her fears, coming out sideways as anger, would dog me the whole trip, because it had happened before, even though I hoped that maybe she had grown beyond this behavior. Back to one of our AA teachings, that "fear is the chief activator of all our character defects." Knowledge does not necessarily make things easier to swallow, just easier to understand.

There was also the disappointment of not being with me for whatever transpired during the trip, so there was no point in arguing. I understood these factors, plus all my own misgivings that I had expressed to her during the weeks leading up to now.

Chapter 4
The Trip

Sunday, September 30- Day 1

Todd said he would be in Lithopolis by ten in the morning and park in the former Bay's IGA grocery store parking lot. I would drive my stuff down to the RV and drop it off, return home, then walk back and we would be ready. Tammy had left for the Sunday Breakfast AA Meeting in Lancaster at 8 AM, and we had stoically said our, "goodbyes, be safe, call, see you in a week and a half." Not wanting to cause a delay, I drove down the street a little before 9:30 AM and saw a large tri-color swirl designed motor home in the parking lot. The question of, "Is that Todd, or could it be someone else?" briefly ran through my mind. It is not like we get a lot of huge motor homes parking randomly around town, so I concluded it had to be him. The last time I had seen Amy's RV was almost a year ago, which is why I was not positive at first. Todd was checking things around the vehicle when I pulled up. We exchanged greetings and then I unloaded my stuff on the pavement and told him I would be back in five minutes to help him load.

It was a sunny, comfortable walk back down the street and promised to be another warm autumn day in Ohio. Upon arriving back at the RV, I discovered a trait in Todd that I would appreciate throughout the next week and a half—he is efficient and organized. All my stuff was already in the RV. The food was unpacked and put away, and the rest of my stuff was stashed in the back bedroom along with his. It was all so deftly put away I could not find anything. I requested his help locating my bags so they could be brought back up to the living room where I would be sleeping on the couch/hide-a-bed. I also asked him to show me how the toilet worked—water pump switch ON, push flush petal, use water hose to rinse the bowl, then pump switch OFF. "Okay, got it!" I said.

Todd was still fiddling around with stuff, so I informed him I was going to the gas station to get coffee and asked if he wanted anything. He still had coffee from home. Then I asked him if he had found a road atlas. "No, I looked but didn't find one. Besides," he added with an air of confidence, "I have a smartphone and a satellite navigation thing I can hook up to it, which I have never used, so we should be good!"

Returning with my coffee, Todd asked, "Are you ready to go?"

"I'm ready, are you?"

"I've been ready!" he declared.

"Well, with all the fiddling around you've been doing, I wasn't sure," I said, then added as he headed toward the driver seat, "I have a favor to ask. Since I have never driven this thing, is it okay if I start driving here? I would rather get acclimated to this beast on roads I know."

"Be my guest!" Todd replied as he motioned toward the captain's chair.

Settling into the high-back leather seat, with armrests, I acclimated myself to the seat adjustment controls, checked controls for wipers, lights, and visibility in the side-view mirrors.

"Hey," I asked, "are these mirrors electric?"

"I think so," Todd responded. "There is something by your left knee that looks like mirror controls. Also, you can adjust the steering wheel with this thing," he added while reaching for a lever on the side of the steering column. Sure enough, the mirrors could be adjusted. Having the mirrors adjusted correctly is very important when driving a car, and absolutely critical to the safe handling of a truck, bus, or large motorhome like this. I spent over a minute getting the mirrors to where I felt I had the best side lane vision, at which point I was feeling much better about driving the huge vehicle already. This motorhome was also equipped with a rearview camera, and the color monitor was on the dashboard.

Very handy to have when backing up or to see if someone is tailgating.

"Okay, Todd, I am going to drive around the parking lot just to see how this thing steers, and then back into a space to make sure I'm seeing what I am supposed to see."

"Do what you need to do!" Todd replied as he rearranged stuff on the console between us.

I was surprised, and pleased, how sharply the big Southwind would turn, and I backed it down between the painted stripes in the lot and stopped right about where I wanted it. Feeling even better!

"All right! Got my coffee, smokes, ashtray, sunglasses, and a bottle of water—I am ready to roll! How about you?"

"Let's roll!" Todd exclaimed.

"One more test," I said as we came to the stop sign at Columbus Street. "I want to see how hard this thing will stop when I really mash on the brakes, so hang on!" The lumbering beast slowed down, but stuff did not go flying forward inside. "Okay! It handles just like a loaded truck! It does not stop worth a crap! I shall make a note of that and adjust accordingly!" I said with a laugh.

"Yeah, that is kinda what I thought too," Todd drolly replied, while messing with his seat.

odometer reading: 45,147 miles at start
10:00 AM sunny 55°F expected high in mid 80s

We turned on to Columbus Street and headed west. "So, what is your plan? Are you figuring we head west on I-70?" I asked as I wheeled through the roundabout at Lithopolis Road and Gender Road.

"Yeah, that's what I was thinking. It goes in the right direction! I looked on Google the other day and that is how we get started," Todd responded, while still trying to get his seat adjusted.

"Seventy West it is, captain! Just wanted to make sure I knew where I was going," I replied. "By the way, how much have you driven this thing?"

"Oh, about fifty miles," Todd responded from behind me while he was rooting around in the kitchen cabinets trying to find the snacks he had stowed away.

"Well," I thought to myself, "I'll have more time than that by the time we stop for fuel."

However, I knew this was only part of the story. Todd retired as a crane operator for All-Crane less than a year ago, and he now had two part-time jobs. One was driving semi-trucks for FedEx, pulling double trailers. His other part-time job was as a substitute bus driver for Circleville Schools, so he was well versed, and had a lot of practice driving large vehicles. He also had spent the previous week and a half working on this RV and knew its systems well. I had an understanding of its various components but had never actually operated them.

Todd brought up the fact that we would need to figure out why the generator would not stay running, so as not to run the batteries down at night. I thought he had fixed it with the new fuel pump, but he said that did not last long and the unit would shut down after less than a minute of running. The generator power was necessary to run the water pumps, heater and air conditioning units, the microwave, the refrigerator, and of course, the interior lights. The refrigerator could be switched to LP (liquid propane) operation, and the furnace used propane as well, but it needed an electric blower. So, having a fully functioning generator was critical for us to be able to live in the RV for this trip. These were some of the things we discussed as we rolled west.

It was getting warmer, and a nice day for traveling. We continued down the Interstate at over seventy miles an hour, smashing more than our fair share of the Midwest insect population on the huge vertical windshield. By now, we had gotten used to the pronounced swaying motion this vehicle exhibited when changing lanes or going into curves. These vehicles get the moniker "land yacht" legitimately, for it felt like being in a boat in choppy water.

Todd was lurching around inside, looking for various things to eat or drink, use the bathroom, rearrange items that had all ended up piled in the master bedroom, messed around with the reclining features of his passenger-side captain's chair some more, and played with his phone. I thought he was just getting things located and squared away since this was the start of the trip. It did not take long to figure out that Todd messed around with stuff all the time, almost as if he needed to continually burn off nervous energy.

Periodically we talked about various aspects of our lives, or AA, or people we had known over the years. Sometimes we remarked about the scenery. We also made a lot of derogatory remarks about other drivers, which became a running joke as the trip wore on. Spot the worst driver, or a potential bad driver, and come up with the most crudely inventive things to say about them. We had a thing or two to say about the horrible condition of the road pavement in Indiana as well. Mostly, though, I just drove. I was enjoying myself more with each passing mile.

As we approached Indianapolis, I asked, "Hey, Todd, do we stay on I-70 straight through town, or do we need to get on the outerbelt?"

"Let's just roll straight through," he replied.

"The only reason I asked, is because I remember something about getting off I-70 and heading to Davenport, Iowa, as one of the ways to go," I observed.

"Yeah, I saw that too. Amy said something about that route as well. Are we close to Iowa or the Mississippi River?"

"Hardly!" I exclaimed, "First we have to go across the rest of Indiana, and then Illinois!"

"All right. Well, let's stay on I-70 for now," he replied. As we rolled through Indianapolis, Todd observed he did not think the city looked so great, but he had been there for basketball playoffs and that part of town was okay.

"So, do you have any idea how long you want to stay on 70?" I asked, returning to the main subject.

"Can we get to the Pacific Ocean on it?" was Todd's response.

"Nope, this road does not make it to the ocean! It does go through Denver, and through the Rockies in Colorado, but it ends somewhere in Utah if I recall correctly. Then you make a right and head for Salt

Lake City and figure out a way to get to Oregon from there!" I replied.

"I really have no desire to go to Utah! Do you?" Todd remarked.

"What's the matter? You have something against Mormons?"

"I don't know! Do you want to go check out some Mormons? We can if you want!"

"Not really!" I replied. "To be honest, though, I think we need a map!"

The pavement improved. We were now in Illinois. It was still sunny and hot, in the mid 80°s, and around midafternoon. Todd suggested we pull off and get fuel since we were just above a quarter of a tank. I got off at the next exit and found a small modern traveler fuel stop, with the end pump island unoccupied. This made maneuvering much easier, but the RV took up the whole area and stuck out partway into the entrance driveway. That was the best I could do and still allow Todd to reach the rear fuel door with the pump nozzle. Fueling was his job since he had the debit card that Amy had loaded with money. I got out and took a picture, then went into the travel store. We also did not have any emergency reflector triangles in case the RV broke down on the road, so I looked for those, and a Rand McNally Road Atlas. They had one regular atlas left, and a special laminated spiral-bound Truckers Atlas, that highlighted all the truck routes and low clearance areas. It was impressive, but for $80, way too expensive for our purposes, so I got the standard version Rand McNally. The store did not have any safety triangles, so that would be something to get later. We both got our insulated travel mugs refilled with nasty coffee and headed back out to the RV. It was time to switch drivers, which meant moving all our personal stuff around so it would be easy to reach. I also brought my camera up to the passenger seat so I could shoot photos through the windshield of anything that caught my eye.

252 miles driven since Lithopolis
4.5 miles per gallon of gasoline!

Day 1 *Todd removes smashed bugs from the driver's side of the windshield at our first fuel stop at I-70 Exit #147 at Route 1 in Marshall, Illinois.*

Before we took off, I checked the Rand McNally. "Hey, Todd, guess what?"
"What?"
"Well, if we were planning to take the cutoff to Davenport, Iowa, we should have done it back in

Indianapolis. We should have taken the outerbelt, then I-74 and headed northwest," I explained.

"So, what do you suggest?" he replied, with renewed interest in this navigation problem.

"I really do not like the idea of backtracking, especially since we are in Illinois now. However, the next Interstate that will take us in the correct northerly direction is all the way across Missouri at Kansas City!"

"I don't want to backtrack either," he replied. "So if we stay on I-70, where does it take us again? And is it the right direction?"

"It is more in the right direction than the two Interstates we will cross between here and Saint Louis, which go northeast then north. We want to go west and northwest, and I-70 will not hit an Interstate like that until we hit Kansas City!" I replied.

"Will we go across the Mississippi River? I want to see the Mississippi!"

"Then I-70 West it is! We will cross the river at St. Louis. Then we have to go clear across the state of Missouri to Kansas City before we pick up the next road, which will be sometime tonight," I cautioned, hoping that by repeating it, my co-driver was clear we had already made a costly mistake in terms of time and miles to drive.

"I'm good! I can drive forever!" Todd declared confidently.

I settled into the passenger seat and stared out a bug-smeared windshield as Todd roared back on to the Interstate. His side was clean. I made a note to myself—point taken. I have to assert a more active role in the fuel-stop procedures as well as learn the other functions of the vehicle. This journey was not going to be about giving directions, but about collaboration, which is an action, rather than passively going along with whatever came my way. I am totally fine with taking action but had held back because I was not sure what, if any, boundaries there may or may not be. The RV was in his possession at the start of this trip, which bequeathed a measure of authority over its operation, and my place in the pecking order. Cleaning the windshield was something I could do and should not have to be asked. Helping with other things would be the least I could do until I learned how to do them myself. This is a basic premise of life in a social setting, at least as far as I am concerned. I needed to practice that behavior on this trip instead of standing back and hoping for instructions.

As the Transportation Manager at Mid-Ohio Foodbank, I had spent years giving direction to my drivers and team, but also had been repeatedly admonished to not stray into areas that were not my responsibility. I sometimes regard incompetence as a vacuum. If something is vital to the functioning of the whole, and those responsible were not taking care of it, I would offer a solution. Usually, my offer would be ignored because it involved another department, or the individual could not execute the process. On a number of occasions, I would go ahead and fix it, or create a process to by-pass the deficiency. Such actions were much to the chagrin of my supervisors, but often to the relief of many of my co-workers. My mantra became, "There are boundaries—they are invisible and moving, but there are boundaries!" When I stepped into a void that I knew was supposed to be someone else's responsibility, I just proceeded to fix things in order to make all our lives easier. Later, when a manager asked, "Who does that?" and the answer came back, "Fred does it," the response would be "Why are you doing that? It's not your responsibility!" My reply would be, "Because no one else was doing it, or they were too incompetent to do it right and it needed to be done." On this trip, I would again be stepping into the voids, but I would also do it in a more collaborative spirit. I welcomed the opportunity to be a full partner in this venture. My earlier trepidations were melting away rapidly.

Now that Todd was driving, it was my chance to wander around the inside of an RV rolling down the highway. I have been on boats of various sizes, but this was more like being on a passenger train speeding along marginal railroad tracks. It took quick reactions and balance to not slam into a wall or fall face first into the furniture as the motorhome lurched and swayed along the road. Taking a leak was a major challenge in both balance and aim. I tried jotting down my first thoughts of the trip in my journal and the initial sentences were almost illegible due to the vehicle motion, but after a while, I sort of got the hang of it. Fixing a peanut butter and jelly sandwich seemed like it would be a task best tackled once I achieved better balance, or when the vehicle was stopped. Peeling and eating a grapefruit, along with a chocolate chip cookie, would have to suffice for a late afternoon snack. It was the only food items I had which could be consumed without making a major mess, or cause injury to myself. Breakfast was the last meal I had, so I was definitely hungry.

I gave Tammy a call and let her know I had been driving all the way to Illinois, which is why she had not heard from me earlier. She asked how driving was, and I told her the RV was actually good to drive and all my fears were for naught. The unknown had been met and it turned out to be nothing. Just fear, and not reality, and assured her everything was just fine. I was at ease now, and I hoped that would put her at ease as well. When told of our routing error due to the lack of a map, and that we were now hell-bent for Saint Louis and Kansas City., Tammy's response was, "How did you let that happen?"

"Well, you put two alcoholics in an RV and tell them to go west. We are going west, and we are making great time! The fact we're not where we should be is a minor detail! We plan to make a correction in Kansas City," I replied with confidence.

"You guys are nuts! This really has turned into *Pee Wee's Big Adventure*!" was Tammy's response, adding, "Be careful!"

The *Pee Wee's Big Adventure* remark was a reference to a movie starring Pee Wee Herman, of the *Pee Wee's Playhouse* television show from the late 1980s. Tammy liked them both. During one of our discussions several days before I left, she had declared that putting Todd and I together sounded like the trip was becoming more like *Pee Wee's Big Adventure* than the straightforward delivery of an RV across the country that it started out as. It was our inside joke.

We crossed the Mississippi River and Todd was duly impressed with its size. We also got a glimpse of the Gateway Arch to the south, in downtown Saint Louis. The freeway wound around through the northern industrial part of the city, with old brick row houses, many burned out and vacant, along with ancient brick factories and warehouses. The area appeared to have been down on its luck for many decades, but I found the old 1800s architecture very interesting. Suburban Saint Louis stretched on for miles and it seemed to take almost an hour before we returned to truly rural landscape, which consisted of mostly tree-covered rolling hills and valleys.

Gently rolling Midwest I-70 westbound in Missouri, viewed through bug splats on the windshield. **Day 1**

The sun was getting low and we were quite hungry by now, so we got off I-70 at Kingdom City, Missouri, which is not quite halfway across the state, and a little east of Columbia. The exit said, "Gateway to the Ozarks." In truth, the Ozark Mountains were about 100 miles to the southwest, but that did not deter the erection of several huge Ozark souvenir stores and outdoor sports equipment retailers. We pulled into a Petro Truck Stop at 7:30 PM

This truck stop was gigantic, and formidable competition to the tourist traps across the highway. The front fuel islands were for automobiles and tourists. The side parking lot was for trucks and trailers and RVs. The backlot had the truck fuel islands, more truck parking, and a truck and trailer repair shop. In the middle of all this was a 1980s era modern building of angled rooflines, fake stone, and slanted windows, housing a huge travel store, a laundromat, and showers for the over-the-road truckers, restrooms, and an Iron Skillet Restaurant. The eating options ranged from a dinner buffet, desert buffet, salad bar, make-your-own pizza station, and lord knows what else—or one could sit down, order from a menu and be served by a waitress. I ordered Cajun-style blackened Tilapia fish, and Todd got the 28-ounce steak. The fish was probably the best I have ever had, moist and tender with a fine spicy flavor. Apparently, the steak was good as well because Todd inhaled it in about three minutes! Mission accomplished—a good meal and a needed pause in the ten-hour driving action.

The sun had just set, yet the temperature was still in the 80°s as we rolled out of the Petro and continued west on I-70. When I asked Todd how long he planned to drive, he stated he could drive all night, but at the very least he wanted to be well on the way up the next Interstate.

"Suit yourself," I said, "but there is no reason to kill yourself! We've done well for one day, and besides, it is not like we are getting paid to do this."

"You got that right!" Todd replied, "No, I would really like to get out of the Midwest and start to see the West tomorrow."

"I do not think that will be a problem, since we are only a couple of hours away from Kansas and the prairie," I remarked.

"Good! Maybe that is what we will see when we wake up!"

"Hopefully not Kansas!" I replied. "If we wake up in Kansas it means we missed another Interstate! Maybe Iowa or Nebraska."

"That would be good," Todd said while nodding in agreement.

We barreled on through the darkness, occasionally talking about personal things, sharing more bits and pieces of our lives. But mostly we rolled in silence, punctuated by profane shouts at stupid drivers who would pass, then slow down in front of us, or who would stay out in the passing lane and go too slow. The game and theme of "berate the idiot" was reaching new levels.

Kansas City was a maze of tight turns and confusing signage, so we were glad we were going through on a Sunday night with little traffic. There was a by-pass, or outerbelt, but the map indicated it would be more direct to go into downtown before getting on Interstate 29 and heading north. Todd continued driving until around 10 PM when he pulled off into a roadside rest area close to Dearborn, Missouri.

"You don't mind staying at a roadside rest area, do you?" he asked.

"No, I'm here for the full experience of life on the road, and this is part of it!" I wearily declared. We had driven a little over 700 miles, just shy of the distance from Columbus to Boston, so it was no wonder we were tired.

As it turned out, we had parked beside a refrigerated semi and the reefer engine was humming in the background. The reefer did drown out some of the highway traffic noise. Todd tried to fire up our generator, but it was not co-operating, so there were no lights, no water, no nothing. Todd left the RV engine running, hoping that it would charge the auxiliary batteries. We prepared our respective sleeping areas using flashlights. Todd showed me a heavy comforter he had bought at Salvation Army. He was not going to use it since there was another one in the master bedroom. I brought a sheet and had purchased a new blanket at Walmart, which was still in the original packaging. I opted to use the comforter since it was ready to go. The sofa looked to be regular size, but it turned out to be much smaller, so small in fact that it was impossible for me to stretch out without my feet hanging over the side, and I am rather short. Uncomfortable though it was, I was too tired to care, but I did seem to toss and turn most of the night. Several times I woke up because I was too hot, and once when the reefer unit on the trailer beside us went into defrost mode with a loud racket, but otherwise, exhaustion made sleep possible.

People with sound minds would think this was an inauspicious start of a lunatic errand. Todd and I, however, were rather pleased to be on the road and making progress, costly detour due to no map and a malfunctioning generator notwithstanding. We were two guys with positive attitudes doing something neither of us had ever done before. Whatever happened next, we would deal with as it presented itself. Neophytes though we were, we were not totally ignorant, nor without some decent life-skills and technical abilities. Little did we know that the no map miscalculation, and the resulting major detour from the most logical route, would present a freedom loaded with unlimited possibilities, none of which would have seemed remotely feasible had we not gone so far astray. That realization would come following a much-needed rest. This trip was beginning to have all the makings of quite an adventure.

Chapter 5
The Badlands

Monday – October 1- Day 2

I woke up around 5 AM, which is fairly normal for me. I was feeling rather slimy and was about to go to the rest area restroom to wash up in the sink when Todd woke up as well. He got the generator running, and it continued running for more than the thirty-second performance last night, so we had water and lights. We got cleaned up and made coffee, and then the generator died again. As it turned out, the restroom was closed due to no water, so it was good we were in an RV, and even better that the generator ran long enough for us to prepare for the day. I went outside to drink my coffee and smoke a cigarette. The air was calm and a very comfortable 65°. All was quiet, except for the traffic on the Interstate. The eastern sky was beginning to brighten. "This is all right!" I thought while being enveloped in the serenity of the moment.

There was no point hanging around, so at 6:45 AM we continued north on I-29 with Todd at the wheel. I called Tammy to give her a progress report and noted how beautiful the red dawn was, and that the landscape looked like Ohio.

"All you can talk about is the red sky and how much fun you are having and not even thinking about me! If it looks like Ohio, you should be here looking at the sunrise from home!" Tammy shouted back.

"Well, if I was not thinking about you, I would not have called," I replied, perplexed, but not totally surprised by the sudden wrath of my dear wife. The conversation continued like this for another minute or so, but by now I was not paying attention and was more interested in concluding the call without any further damage.

"Tammy not happy?" Todd deadpanned from the driver seat.

"Not one bit," I replied.

"Sorry to hear that, brother."

We rolled north on I-29 and soon encountered rain and fog, and the temperature started to fall. I was glad I had put long pants on when I got up in the morning, and now it was time for a sweatshirt. Periodically we could see the Missouri River over to the left, but for the most part, we were too far away to see it. The highway was in the valley, but it was broad and flat, not a steep valley like river valleys in Ohio. The hills to either side were much farther away and lower.

Twenty or thirty miles north of Council Bluffs, Iowa we stopped at a remote truck stop to fuel up and get breakfast. There was a heavy soaking drizzle falling out of the sky, and it was windy. The temperature had dropped to 50°, so it was not pleasant at all. This truck stop was a small local affair, located at US-30 / Lincoln Highway, near Missouri City, Iowa. It had a gravel parking lot for trucks and a small diner called The Cornstalk Cafe attached to the convenience store. Locals hung out there as well as travelers, so eavesdropping on conversations was interesting and varied. Mostly the talk was about the weather and the fact that summer was definitely over. Pictures lined the walls showing the place back in the mid-1990s when there was a major flood on the Missouri, which put four feet of water on the fuel island, and three feet of water inside the diner, even though the river was about two miles away.

Todd was trying to talk his way through the generator problem while we waited for our breakfast. The best he could figure was that it seemed to be a fuel issue. He noted that several times he found the fuel line in the jerry-can stuck to the side. I hazarded the guess that the fuel pump was working just fine, and that the rubber fuel line was getting stuck to the side of the can by suction, and that a solution might be to cut two angles at the end of the rubber hose so it could not suck itself to the side, or even cut a notch in the tube about an inch and a half above the end so the fuel pump would be drawing from there instead of only from the end. Todd liked the idea.

I changed the subject to something he had mentioned before the trip started, and that was that he wanted to see the west.

"So, do you have anything in particular you would like to see while we're out here?"

"I don't know," he replied hesitantly, "there's so much, and I want to see some of it."

"I agree."

"What would you like to see?" Todd responded, and thereby turned the tables.

"The Grand Canyon! But we will be nowhere close to that. Also, I have always thought The Badlands would be cool to see," I replied.

"Are you sure we can't get to Grand Canyon?" he asked as he looked at me quizzically.

"Oh, anything is possible! But it is way the hell over in Arizona, and we would need to change our direction right now, and head southwest. You would need to call Amy for a lot more fuel money!"

"That's not happening!" he smirked. "What about The Badlands?"

"I think it can be sort of on the way, and that would put us in position to possibly go to Yellowstone as well. I'll check the map," I said.

"Cool!" was his expansive response.

The waitress returned with our breakfast order and refilled our coffee cups. I was still working on the first half of my stack of blueberry pancakes when Todd looked up from his now empty plate that previously contained eggs, bacon, and hash brown potatoes, and announced, "I'm going out to work on the fuel line for the generator. No rush, you take your time." I felt a bit guilty not going out in the rain to help him, but I was not going to abandon half a plate of blueberry pancakes either, so I continued to enjoy my breakfast and the snippets of conversation as the waitresses bantered with the customers.

Finished with my leisurely brunch, I wandered out the side door and lit a smoke. One of the waitresses was leaning against the building while having a smoke of her own and trying to stay out of the blowing drizzle. We exchanged small talk while I scanned the gravel lot for Todd and our RV. I thought I heard someone yell, then yell again, and finally detected Todd motioning for me.

"You ready to roll?" he asked.

"Yup!" I replied.

"I cut notches in the fuel line like you suggested. See?! And I have run the generator three times and it does not quit. We should be able to have lights and heat tonight," Todd said with satisfaction.

"Great!" I replied. "That is good news!"

As we continued up the Iowa side of the Missouri River, the rain let up for the most part. The land was low and swampy, with large drainage and irrigation ditches going off in various directions. Things looked fairly green like the rest of the Midwest, but the topography was definitely not like Ohio. The land was changing. I also noticed that the rear of the RV was smelling like sewer gas since we left the roadside rest, and it was getting more powerful and obnoxious as the morning wore on.

Todd worked his cellphone while he was driving. First, a call to Margy to see how she was doing and to let her know where we were. His son Noah was to go for his driver's license test this week, so there was some discussion about making sure his head was wrapped around what he needed to do for that, and what paperwork he needed to have, but the actual appointment arrangements were to be executed by Michelle, Todd's ex-wife and his son's mother. Next, he called Noah, who was surprised that Todd was not home. Being a teenager, the whole concept that the large RV which had been sitting in the driveway for several weeks while being prepared for a trip, and was now gone, meant that his father was gone as well had entirely eluded him. I could relate to the dissociation of the obvious in the mind of a teenager, for I had dealt with that with our son Jason. So there were reminders to Noah to let his school know he would be absent to not jeopardize his player status for the Friday night football game and attending the homecoming dance, make sure he found his lost paperwork, and that his mother, Michelle, would be going with him. The next call was to his mother. Todd had briefly considered bringing her along on this trip, but that got nixed for some reason, and he talked like she should know me, even though I never recall having met the woman. All the calls ended with, "I love you." They reminded me of how busy one's life gets with children involved, and my gratitude for now being retired and not having to deal with any of that even though Tammy and I hear about the busyness with all our grandkids activities. It just did not seem that way when I was growing up. My brother and I had bicycles and bus tickets to get us where we needed to go, and it was our responsibility.

I-29 returned to the riverside as we went through Sioux City, Iowa, and then swung north into South Dakota and the topography flatted out. An electronic overhead sign welcomed all to the state, gave a reminder to drive safe, and ended with the declaration of "Dilly Dilly". Todd and I looked at each other and shrugged, being totally clueless as to what that meant. I called Tammy to give her a progress report, and let her know we were still alive, but based on the call earlier in the morning, I doubted she really cared. She was civil and thanked me for letting her know where we were. That was a relief.

The speed limit had increased to 80 miles per hour, and our new goal was to get to I-90 and head west across South Dakota toward The Badlands. Sioux Falls, South Dakota looked like the last city of any size that we would hit, so we got off at an exit there to look for some kind of store that might sell something to fix the sewer gas problem. All we encountered was a retail mall with a Target Store across from it. Driving a vehicle of this size, wandering around an unknown city can lead to tight situations that we might not get out of, so Todd chose the Target. It was a long shot, and we came up empty-handed.

Flat southeastern South Dakota, on I-29, speed limit 80 mph but not in the RV. **Day 2**

I-90 westbound, west of Sioux Falls, South Dakota. Gently rolling grassland, and steadily climbing. **Day 2**

We changed drivers, and I guided our rolling behemoth out of Sioux Falls and back to the Interstate. Within a few miles, we came to a sprawling interchange and headed west on I-90. The topography changed immediately to abrupt round hills and wide valleys. It was very peculiar in appearance and almost looked like an illustration from a *Doctor Seuss* book. Familiar Midwest trees quickly disappeared, and all became grassland. At last, the land looked different and strange to us. This was the West. Aspen and elder trees grew along the creeks and around the many kettle lakes formed after the last Ice Age, but those were now the only trees on the landscape. It also became obvious that we were slowly and continuously climbing. The vistas became broader and the horizon more distant. The land was sparsely populated, occasionally punctuated by small agricultural villages dominated by large grain silos and elevators, many of which had excess grain piled in huge mounds right on the ground.

Half the crossroads along this stretch of I-90 were single-lane gravel roads leading to nowhere, and those were about ten to fifteen miles apart. Road signs announced towns that were miles and miles away, and not visible. Either the towns were really sparsely scattered across the state or the route of the Interstate intentionally missed them all. The farther we went, the more I had the sense that there were no towns, just the signs. Really big billboards, however, were not a rarity out here, and there were definitely a lot of them. Most were touting the wonders of Wall Drug, in Wall, South Dakota. If the billboards were to be believed, this place had everything, and it was barely three hundred miles away, then only two hundred sixty miles, and so on, but the only thing I recall was the coffee for 5 cents per cup. There also was a fire museum somewhere, and as we progressed west, each of the huge billboards were accompanied by a firetruck. I was starting to wonder if most of the retired firetrucks in the United States were finding their way to these signs along the road as the number of them increased. Occasionally a sign would declare that there was an "authentic re-creation" of a frontier town ahead, which sounded like an oxymoron to me. It featured cowboys and Indians, plus gunfights, so for a van loaded with bored kids, this could be a memorable diversion. So, there were actual signs extolling wonders to behold just ahead, yet the expansive rolling landscape contained fewer and fewer signs of civilization by the mile. Fewer towns, fewer fences, fewer houses, fewer power lines, to the point that the only signs of human life out here seemed to be the giant billboards themselves.

Due to the distance between visible towns, our new strategy was to not let the fuel level go much below half a tank, so we got off I-90 near a town called Kennebec, which had been detected for several miles by the large grain storage facility and the cluster of trees. There was a small cinderblock gas station halfway between the exit ramp and the town. The pump was running slow, so I took a few pictures before cleaning the windshield. Inside the gas station, there was one pot of coffee, a restroom, and an odd assortment of snacks and travel supplies. As luck would have it, they did carry an RV sewage holding tank disinfectant, so we got a bottle of that and Todd dumped about a quarter of it down the toilet. That improved the quality of the air in the RV significantly, leaving only the acrid odor of exhaust fumes once we were back motoring down the road.

Kennebec, South Dakota, fuel stop off I-90. Large grain elevators in the distance, rising above the town hidden by short trees in a low valley about half a mile away. **Day 2**

Around 5 PM we crossed into Mountain Time. By now it had been mostly sunny for several hours, but still cool. I pulled off at a marked scenic overlook, wanting to see the real west. There was nothing to see except for short wheat-colored grass covering the undulating landscape that extended dozens of miles to the horizon. One scraggly tree was visible in a swale miles away. In a way, it was stunning in its nothingness. In Ohio, a big valley may be a quarter to half a mile across, while being able to see something fifteen miles away is rather impressive. Out here in the West, the expansive view is almost incomprehensible. I called Tammy one more time, since I had a signal, and woke her up. I apologized, told her we were doing fine, that we currently were literally looking at nothing, and had also crossed another time zone. I added that we were probably going to end the day somewhere near the Badlands, because there was a KOA Campground advertised there. She groggily thanked me for the update.

View from the scenic overlook along I-90 in north-central South Dakota, west of Kennebec. It seemed like the horizon was just on the edge of infinity.

Todd took over driving after the scenic stop. He was probably afraid I would stop at another one to see if it was better. It was another hour or so before we got off at Exit 131 and headed south on RT-240 to Badlands National Park. There was no one in the guard shack so we rolled on down the road into the park. Cresting the edge of a hill the land changed from the scrub grass to a valley of light-colored rock sculptures in bizarre shapes.

From grasslands to The Badlands. South Dakota. **Day 2**

"Beware Rattlesnakes" sign along Badlands trail in Badlands National Park

Badlands National Park, endless eroded bentonite which seemed to change shape and color depending on how the light played upon the strange forms.

Jagged spires and strange shapes in Badlands

I shot a whole roll of film at the first overlook. The jagged pinnacles, spires, and narrow valleys were carved out by erosion. As the sun moved in and out from behind clouds the light changed the whole appearance of the other-world-like landscape. The size of the first formations seemed small and compressed in comparison with the vast landscape vistas we had encountered most of the afternoon, with the peaks only a couple of hundred feet high, but impressive and indescribable, nevertheless. We stopped at another pull-off and followed a trail through one of the chasms and came out the other side to a surface marred by a jumble of cuts and crevasses. The sun was starting to set, and we needed to find a place to park for the night, so we hurried back to the RV and continued down the road while gawking at the unfolding sights at every turn. The further we drove, the deeper the chasms became, and the higher the strange formations rose above us. My first impression of the small scale of the features and the extent of them across the landscape had been wiped out by more experience with the place. It is truly impressive and beguiling, and I was glad we had made the effort to get here, for it was all that I had hoped for and more.

Surreal landscape silhouette in the Badlands, South Dakota.
Day 2

The Badlands rising out of the grassland south of the main park area, near Interior SD, in the late evening sun. **Day 2**

Exiting the park, a little past 6 PM, we drove a short distance to a dusty hamlet named Interior, South Dakota. It was located in a kind of broad valley, or basin, with the north wall being the sculpted moonscape we had just driven down through. The southern wall could be seen glowing far away in the sunset. It appeared to be more of the same, but probably fifteen or twenty, miles away. The rocks were dried bentonite clay and gravel, and the valley floor was pocked by large mounds or hillocks of the same stuff. Our objective at Interior was to get on another road and go to the KOA Campground. Other than the very small village, the whole area seemed totally desolate, yet out of nowhere, a speeding beat-up white Ford pickup truck materialized and blew past us.

Todd drolly remarked, "Dad-burn Indians wearing cowboy hats, and driving like crazy people!"

Much later, while scrutinizing one of the many maps I had collected along our journey, I discovered we were on the northern edge of the Pine Ridge Indian Reservation, home of the Oglala Lakota Sioux Tribe. The hat-wearing men in the speeding pickup truck were probably upset that a large RV, being driven by two old white guys, was taking up most of the road. We were invading their home; they were not interrupting the serenity of ours. A little over fifty miles due south is Wounded Knee, site of one of the most heinous chapters of white "Manifest Destiny" when U.S. Army Calvary soldiers massacred upward of 300 Native Americans, including at least 60 women and children, with four rapid-fire Hotchkiss guns, on December 29, 1890. We might have comported ourselves a bit more respectfully, had we known, but more to the point is that the remark should not have been the first reaction. This hardscrabble land is where the First Americans of the plains tribes have been forced to live for over one hundred years. From a land of freedom and plenty to confinement in desolation.

We crossed a bridge over the White River, and in the fading light, it was obvious the name was appropriate because the water looked like milk due to the clay sediment in the stream. Scrubby trees grew along the so-called river, but the rest of the landscape was the same short course grass and sage we had been encountering for the past several hours. We spotted the KOA sign and pulled in the drive. The gate was closed and locked. A handwritten sign was wired to the gate, stating, "Closed for the winter!"

"Well, Todd, guess we're not going to experience the comfort of a KOA tonight! I wonder when winter starts?"

"Apparently yesterday! Look, the date at the bottom of the sign says September 30! That's yesterday!"

"Dang! So close!" I replied, then added, "We passed a funky looking RV park back there in Interior. We probably should find out if they are open, or if they have wimped out for the winter as well. I think we are rapidly running out of options!"

"Yeah, I'll try to swing this baby around, and hope I don't hit any speeding Indians!" Todd retorted. The sun was setting, and the western sky was an appealing orange-yellow, then red, with the light fading fast.

Downtown Interior, South Dakota, in the golden evening light. A bentonite hillock marks the end of the street.

We were in luck! The Badlands RV Park & Motel was open! The lanky gentleman behind the counter assigned us a spot, then informed us there was no water or sewer hookup, but there was electric and a shower house. That sounded just fine, and the location was great. The Badlands to the north and east were still glowing in the fading sunset. Todd operated the three slide-outs on the RV and connected the power cable, after getting a pigtail from the office that would match our cord, which was bigger than a dryer cable. This was the first time we would actually use the RV as intended—to live comfortably in it, even if it was just overnight. It sure beat the rest area! We had lights and room to move around inside, plus no truck reefer droning away beside us.

The Badlands RV Park & Motel.

Our RV setup for the full living experience, with the room extension sliders deployed. Badlands RV Park & Motel at Interior, South Dakota. End of **Day 2**

When we fueled earlier in the afternoon, Todd had picked up a frozen DiGiorno's pizza. We tried cooking it in the oven but could not get the gas burners to light. Next, we tried the microwave, which turned out to also be a convection oven, but the buttons on the keypad were indecipherable. Nevertheless, I persisted, and finally got the pizza cooking. Frozen pizza never tasted so good!

Todd brought some movie DVDs for the trip, so we could have some entertainment in the evening. Actually, he brought a lot of stuff for our journey and was prepared for a number of contingencies. Tonight's offering was a Christian spiritually-themed movie titled *Conversations With God."* It was based primarily on the first book of a series by the same title by Neale Donald Walsch, subtitled <u>An Uncommon Dialogue</u>. It was interesting and posed a number of good philosophical points, which we discussed briefly, but we were both too tired to finish the movie or the conversation, so we called it a night.

We had put in a 600-mile day and had traversed a dramatic change in landscape, from lush growth in the Missouri River Valley to the stark beauty of the upper plains to the Moonscape of the Badlands.

Chapter 6
Repairs

Tuesday, October 2- Day 3

At about 2 AM I got up to pee—which is typical for an old guy who stays well-hydrated—when I heard a loud metallic rattling noise coming from the heater blower. It sounded like a tin can stuck in a fan and kept getting louder. I fumbled around in the dark trying to find a flashlight, or a light switch, when the noise went BANG!!! and stopped. Cool air, instead of warm, was blowing out the ceiling unit, and no air was coming out of the heat vent below the kitchen sink, which seemed to be the source of the noise. Next, I went outside to see if there was any evidence of a fire. It was so dark out that any fire or sparks would have easily been observed, and the flashlight I finally found did not shine on any smoke emanating from the furnace vent.

My final check was the amp meter on the hallway control panel. The readings were normal, and I was glad Todd showed me those. Actually, I had no idea what I was looking for or what I was doing, but it was not getting any worse, except for no heat, so I added another blanket and went back to bed.

Waking up to a dim light, I peeked out the curtain and saw it was dawn, which to me means the day has already started and it is time to get moving. I stowed away the hide-a-bed, folded the sheet and blankets, and got ready to go to the shower house. Stepping outside, the eastern sky was turning red and orange, and silhouetting the jagged Badlands peaks in the distance. I grabbed my camera and walked out to the road to get a better view to shoot pictures of the sunrise. It was dead calm and cold. The temperature was around 45°, but it was tolerable due to no wind, though still a shock after the 80° weather in Ohio two days earlier.

Sunrise, Interior, South Dakota, looking at the Badlands to the east. **Day 3**

Wanting to share this experience, I called Tammy but had to leave a message. I then realized she would already be on her way to her sister's house so they could go to jewelry class at the Cultural Arts Center in downtown Columbus, so I called her cellphone, and had to leave another message. I was surprised I was even getting a signal, and disappointed I was not able to tell her where we were and what I was seeing, so I headed back to the RV. Todd was getting up when I walked in. I told him what had happened last night with the noise from the fan and the loss of heat.

Just then, Tammy called back. I gave her an update, including the excitement last night, but her main concern was that we should go to an Indian reservation and buy her some turquoise jewelry. Although I knew we had traveled close to several reservations, the Interstate did not have jewelry stands, and the small town we were currently in did not appear to be a tourist hot spot. None of this mattered, for she was sure I could find some if I looked hard enough, which may have been true. I had to tell her it was not a priority right now.

My priority was to get cleaned up, so I headed to the shower located at the end of the park office. This turned out to be a rather stark affair—all concrete, with a basic cement and plywood shower stall, plus a sink, toilet stall, and a bench to dress upon. It was illuminated by one bare lightbulb, hanging from the ceiling, which gave it just the right ambiance. To top things off, it was unheated, and someone had left the door open overnight. Thankfully, the water was hot, but the shower and shave were definitely brisk.

Nevertheless, it was badly needed, and I felt much better having endured it. This was definitely becoming quite the adventure and pushing me out of my comfort zones. I was feeling invigorated facing the challenge—not that I actually equate a brisk shower with the height of deprivation, but I have grown very accustomed to the creature comforts of home, and this definitely failed that low standard.

Todd fixed himself some fried potatoes with green peppers and onions for breakfast. He offered to share, but I am such a creature of habit that I stuck with my usual bowl of cereal. The next task was to take the furnace apart to diagnose the cause of the racket last night and subsequent loss of heat. The RV had no tools, so I went to the park office to see if there were some we could borrow. The manager, who I now assumed was also the owner of this piece of paradise, was kind enough to take me to his maintenance shop room. I requested a regular and a Phillips head screwdriver. Todd was hoping that would be sufficient to take most of the panel off the heater, and he was correct. Half of the plastic squirrel-cage fan had disintegrated. While the other half was still intact, an airflow sensor kept the furnace from igniting due to low airflow caused by the missing half of the fan. The whole fan assembly would have to be replaced. Little plastic fan fins were scattered throughout the small furnace. We removed the broken pieces the best we could, although we suspected a couple had fallen behind the metal heat-exchanger tubes and were now out of sight and reach. We checked for parts on the laptop computer Todd had brought and then searched for a source to buy one. Rapid City, South Dakota appeared to be our best and only bet. There were several RV and camper dealers listed in the vicinity, but the one place Todd was able to talk to did not have it. Warm weather was now a thing of the past, at least out here it was, so no heat was not a viable option. We had to get this fixed.

I took the tools back to the park office and had told Todd that I intended to buy some postcards, then walk to the Post Office in town to mail them. He was fine with this, for he had some things he wanted to do. When we checked in the night before I had scanned the slim offering of postcards and souvenirs in the park office, so it did not take long to make my selection. I also bought the only Badlands National Park ball hat on the shelf. I spotted that last night as well and thought it looked right handsome and practical. I knew the town was small, for the welcome sign beside the RV park proudly stated the population of Interior, South Dakota was 62, but I thought it best to ask for directions.

"Go down the main street, almost to the end. You can't miss it!" were the manager's classic directions.

There was a gas station where the unmarked "main street" intersected the state road, but the business did not appear to be open. The town was poor and hardscrabble in appearance. Small houses with assorted junk in the yards, two churches, a jail, a school built in 1930 that now functioned as an elementary school, a small park with a hand painted sign touting the rich history of the town, a couple of bars, and a small market with the Post Office attached.

The "main street" was paved, but the several side streets, including an actual Main Street, quickly deteriorated to gravel, and disappeared into the scrub a couple hundred feet away. I exchanged pleasantries with two men standing in a yard and confirmed I was heading in the right direction to the Post Office, then one added, "Watch out for high winds coming tomorrow, and the temperature is going to drop as well!" I thanked them for the advice and headed down the street to complete my mission.

Panoramic view of Interior, South Dakota in the Badlands, behind the trees.

Interior, South Dakota – intersection of Main Street and "the main street."

Vintage bucking bronco ready for the next rider with a quarter and some courage, at the Cowboy Corner, Interior, SD

A tee pee, which could be rented for an overnight stay at The Badlands RV & Motel, Interior, SD.

Todd had moved the RV to the park office and was waiting for me to return. I apologized for holding us up by messing around in the big city, and also informed him about the approach of a drastic change in the weather predicted for tomorrow. We took a scenic drive through more of Badlands National Park, winding through canyons and up and down hills. As we left the park, we found this gate was staffed. The woman wanted us to pay the entrance fee even though we informed her we were leaving. She was not amused but then inquired as to whether we had some kind of pass. After some further discussion, she offered a senior discount for me if I bought a National Park pass good for the rest of the year, and Todd would be no charge. Apparently, she assumed we were father and son. It seemed like a deal for $20 so I gave her the money and thanked her.

Todd looked over to me and said, "Thanks, Dad!" and laughed.

The road left the weird rock formations suddenly, and we found ourselves back up on rolling prairie, populated appropriately enough by a number of prairie dog villages. They were rather cute little creatures, sitting up watching stuff or scurrying around just like in old nature programs on TV. We saw antelope as well. None of the wildlife appeared to be much concerned about a large RV rolling through their midst. The road slowly made its way toward the crest of a high ridge, upon which ran I-90. Across the bridge over the Interstate was Wall, South Dakota, home of the famous Wall Drug, touted by billboards for hundreds of miles. Wall appeared to be no larger than Interior but looked more prosperous because the street was better paved and parking spots were marked along the curbs. We resisted the temptation to get a five-cent cup of coffee at the now infamous drug store, for we were on an urgent mission, and headed west on the Interstate toward Rapid City.

Through numerous phone calls, Todd had located Camper World just west of Rapid City, and not far off I-90. He could not confirm they had the fan, but conversations with other dealers indicated this place was our best bet. As we approached Rapid City, the landscape changed again. The undulating prairie ended abruptly, and hills began. In the distance were larger hills that appeared dark, due to the pine trees covering them. We were at the foothills of The Black Hills, and Rapid City was right on the edge.

Camper World was actually in a suburb west of Rapid City, named Sommerset, and the store with a gigantic American flag flying from an equally large pole, though visible from the Interstate, was down a residential street. This made navigating a large RV between cars, bicycles, and four way-stops a bit of a challenge. We arrived without crushing any Big Wheels or small children. Stepping out of the motor home, we discovered it was 84° with high haze and sun. The last time we had stepped out of our vehicle was back at the Badlands, and it was barely in the 50s. Camper World had one fan blower, for twenty bucks, and they lent us the tools to install it. By 2:30 PM, the job was done.

While the main priority of the day had been to fix the furnace blower, there was sufficient time during the drive from The Badlands to Rapid City to discuss other priorities, like where to go next, philosophy, spirituality, and check-in with the folks back home when there was a cellphone signal. Todd declared that he always wanted to see Mount Rushmore, so after a quick consult with the Rand McNally, I confirmed that such a visit was very possible since it appeared to be only thirty miles southwest of Rapid City. We decided that we should add it to our itinerary once we got the heat problem resolved. I also reminded him that a major detour to Yellowstone National Park ought to be considered as well, since neither one of us would probably ever get this close again, and it could get us back on track toward Oregon. My partner in this adventure was quite receptive to this line of thinking.

I called Tammy and updated her on the successful repair, and informed her we might go to Mount Rushmore, "because it was so close—not far out of town, actually." She was not buying this, because she knows me, and was beginning to suspect Todd and I were probably going to dream up all sorts of places to see that she would like to experience as well. My announcement was received rather coolly. Meanwhile, Todd had been providing additional coaching for his son on taking his driver's exam later in the week and sorting out the logistics for getting Noah to the testing site, with the proper paperwork, and other helpful hints and reminders as well. Todd had done this yesterday but wanted to make sure it all stuck in Noah's teenage brain through repetition. He also checked his home security cameras and noted to Noah that the lawn still needed to be cut. Noah protested, but Todd informed him he was looking at the yard as they spoke. We both started to appreciate the serenity achieved when there was no cellphone signal.

Another thing we agreed upon was that we were definitely hungry. I asked the nice lady at Camper World for dining suggestions.

"There are a lot of places back toward town along the service road. It just depends on what you are interested in," she brightly replied.

"We are not interested in anything fancy. Decent sandwiches, anything!" I said, then added, "By service road, do you mean Sturgis Road, or something else?"

"Oh, yes. Sturgis Road. None of us call it that! There is a nice restaurant at the next exit. A lot of the people here go there for lunch!" she responded cheerily.

"Thank you for the info and thank you for the use of the tools!" I replied.

"Did you get it fixed?" she inquired.

"I don't know about fixed, but there are no parts or pieces left over, so we will find out tonight," I said as I turned for the door.

Todd decided there was no point getting back on the Interstate to go one exit, so he cruised back toward Rapid City on Sturgis Road. There were churches, apartments, auto parts stores, but no places to eat. We passed through the intersection that brought I-90 traffic down from the so-called 'next exit,' but it was not looking any more promising on the eating establishment front than we had already seen, so we got on I-90 and went up one more exit. There was a sign for a diner in a small strip-center of offices, but it looked closed, and there was no place to park an RV. A gas station had a pizza shop attached to it, so Todd pulled in there and quickly found out we were too big to be there as well. It was too late to do anything about it though. He got out and walked behind the building to see if we could go around it. While he was gone, a bread truck came out from behind, followed by a beverage truck. When Todd came back, I remarked that the vendor trucks were getting through.

"Yeah, they got through. It is tight though, and there is one of those little 'casinos' over on the other side! But I think we can make it," he replied. One of the joys of driving a really big vehicle is making sure you do not get stuck somewhere and have to back out blindly.

Little casinos were ubiquitous in our travels around South Dakota. They were in truck stops, big gas stations, and little free-standing buildings. No matter the configuration or location, they were always dark inside, and had a couple of video poker and slot machines blinking merrily from the gloom. It became a running joke for us to spot the strangest looking or weirdly located casinos. One was in a barely disguised former Wendy's restaurant, but most were simply backrooms of other establishments. One or two people would be grimly fixated on the screen of the machine in front of them. These were the total opposite of the flashy crowded casinos in Las Vegas, and definitely lacked floor shows or Elvis impersonators.

Todd extracted the motorhome from the small parking lot, and we did not succumb to the allures of the little casino. For now, not only did we need something to eat we also needed to fuel the RV. It was time to stop messing around, so we got back on I-90 and headed for downtown Rapid City, and the route toward The Black Hills and Mount Rushmore, our thinking being that there had to be fuel and eats on the way to this world-renowned bit of scenic splendor.

The street was five lanes wide, and if we had been driving a Toyota, we could have shot into a number of gas stations or restaurants on either side, but those options were not available to us. Finally, I spotted a Ruby Tuesday restaurant on a corner with a large parking lot dug into the side of a hill.

"Go there!" I yelled.

"Are they any good?" Todd asked.

"Yes," I replied, "But more important, it is on our side of the street and it has a ton of parking, even though it is built into the side of a hill."

There were hardly any cars in the Ruby Tuesday parking lot. When we walked in we discovered there was hardly any staff either. We finally tracked down someone to summon the hostess, a beefy tattooed girl with a ratted pneumatic hairdo that towered about a foot above her head. I had not seen a hairdo like this since the late 1980s. She began dithering about where to seat us.

"It should not be too difficult," I mumbled sarcastically while trying to be helpful as well, "since the place is virtually empty!"

"Easy, brother," Todd admonished me, in a hushed voice.

As it turned out, one waitress was working the whole room, so where we sat did not matter. Soon after we were seated, a couple of other small groups of diners came in and they were shown to tables near us. Apparently, the kitchen was short-staffed as well. Todd ordered something that included a trip to the salad bar, and his salad was long gone before the main meal appeared. It arrived just in time, because Todd had gotten on his smartphone, brought up the Ruby Tuesday website, and was about to order to have his food delivered out to the RV in the parking lot. He was hoping it would be faster than waiting on his meal in the dining room. It was either that, or he was going to make a complaint to the manager by text.

The people in a booth nearby were starting to get restless as well. One of them pantomimed carving up his napkin with a knife and fork and eating it, much to the amusement of all who observed the performance. The food, though late, was great, so we made the mistake of ordering dessert. Again, it took eons to arrive, even after letting the waitress know we were still waiting. Todd ordered some frozen ice cream and chocolate concoction that appeared to be erupting out of a large brandy snifter laying on its side. This elicited "ooo's" and "aahhh's" from the folks in the booth who had been preparing to eat the napkins.

"Don't get too excited," I loudly declared, "he ordered that three hours ago!" This was met with guffaws and knowing smirks. We finally left the restaurant a little after 4 PM

There was not much to Rapid City, even though downtown was comprised of a dozen or more city blocks of two-and three-story buildings. Some were 1960's drab institutional or governmental looking concrete affairs. The rest of the buildings appeared to be less than one hundred years old. There was not an extensive residential area evident either as US-16 began climbing a hill out of town and to a more rural area. After ascending several miles through fields, pine trees, and rock outcroppings, we started encountering all sorts of strange "tourist traps," such as Reptile City, Dino Universe, and Black Bear World, but no gas stations. Finally, one appeared at the top of a hill.

"Better stop here," Todd remarked, "it might be our only chance." Sweatshirts, tee shirts, and ball caps—all touting South Dakota, The Black Hills, Mount Rushmore, Native Americans, and wolves howling at the moon—filled shelves and racks in the large low-ceilinged metal-clad pole building. There was a very small casino in the back. In other words, it was tourist heaven, except there were no tourists. We were the only customers, save for a few locals who wandered in for beer and smokes, while we scoped out the merchandise. Even with this large of a selection, and an end-of-season discount of 50% off, we could not find anything to suit our exacting tastes.

The road to Mount Rushmore, after the tourist traps, became very scenic. Pine-covered jagged mountains with cliffs and other rock outcroppings, along with deep valleys, and a lot of black-tailed deer grazing by the side of the pavement. We went through Keystone, a concentrated tourist mecca crammed into a tight narrow valley, made to look like an old frontier town, but seemed to be fairly new construction. The trinket shops and restaurants in the rustic looking buildings were all closed for the season. It was the same story for most of the new motels and all the RV parks. We pressed on to Mount Rushmore.

The original idea of carving the faces of famous people on a Black Hills cliff was proposed by a South Dakota historian named Doane Robinson. He hoped the outsize likenesses of American West heroes such as Lewis & Clark, Chief Red Cloud, and Buffalo Bill Cody would spur tourism in the area. Sculptor Gutzon Borglum, who had worked on the massive Confederate Memorial carving at Stone Mountain, Georgia was hired for the project. Borglum felt something with broader appeal would be more appropriate, and selected Presidents George Washington, Thomas Jefferson, Abraham Lincoln, and Theodore Roosevelt to be the subjects because of their role in creating, preserving, and expanding the United States.

Federal funding for the project was secured and work began in 1927. The Chief Carver of the mountain was an Italian immigrant named Luigi del Bianco, an artisan and headstone carver from Port Chester, New

York. The work was accomplished by four hundred workers using dynamite to blast 410,000 tons of rock off the cliff before the finish work by hand could be done. The original scope of the sculptures was to be from head to waist, but funding ran out and only the faces were completed. Washington's face was dedicated in 1934, Jefferson's in 1936, and Lincoln in 1937. A 1937 bill was introduced in Congress to add the face of women's voting rights activist Susan B. Anthony, but funding was only approved to complete the existing faces. Teddy Roosevelt's face was dedicated in 1939. Construction continued on a plaza, a museum with a Hall of Records, rubble removal, and finish work on the sculptures themselves. Gutzon Borglum died of an embolism in March 1941. His son, Lincoln, was to proceed with finishing the sculptures down to their waists, but funding quickly dried up and work was halted in October 1941.

Mount Rushmore was selected by Borglum because of its southeast orientation, which allowed for maximum sun exposure, and for its rock stability. Each sculpted head is sixty feet tall. The visitor center was constructed in 1957, and the whole plaza complex was redone in 1998.

It was just after 5 PM when we arrived at the park, which was when they stopped charging admission. The parking lots were mostly empty, so we were able to park the land yacht close to the promenade entrance. The landscaping was tasteful and the stone plaza leading to the overlook was done well too, with a very heroic and patriotic feel to it. The four presidents sculpted in rock at the top of a mountain were about a quarter of a mile away, across a deep ravine, so the true scale was greatly diminished. Due to the late hour, they were now in the shade, so the effect was a bit underwhelming, but the price was right. Nevertheless, Mount Rushmore is impressive and iconic, so we were glad we made the effort to see it.

Stone Plaza leading to Mt. Rushmore   *Promenade of the States at Mount Rushmore, South Dakota.* **Day 3**

Finding a place to stay before nightfall now became imperative. We had seen one private RV park near Keystone that had a few motorhomes parked in it, so we drove there only to find a sign on the gatehouse stating they were closed for winter effective October 1. However, there was a courtesy phone, and a number to call for information. Todd dialed the number. Our hope was that they would allow us to park overnight anyway. No dice, but the lady said there might be a park still open up on Route 385, about eight or ten miles away, called Whispering Pines.

"Let's give it a shot!" Todd declared.

"It doesn't seem like we have much of a choice," I replied.

The sun had dropped below the mountains when we finally located Whispering Pines. An older woman with wild gray hair was standing in the driveway. She was talking to a younger well-dressed man sporting a hip slicked-back haircut and drinking a beer from a long-necked bottle as we pulled in. I was learning more about the RV park subculture. The woman was a resident manager, meaning she stayed for free in her own RV and managed the place. The young businessman owned the park. She assigned us a spot and told me to meet her in the office once we were all hooked up. The man finished his beer and said he was going home to Rapid City.

I helped Todd, then went to the office to pay. The lady invited us to join some of the other residents for the last campfire of the year, over on an outdoor patio. I said we would think about it, but it had been a long day. Then I inquired about the weather. She said a cold front was approaching. The prediction was for high winds up to sixty miles an hour tomorrow, and the temperature would be dropping into the thirties by tomorrow evening. Also, there was a chance of snow. The weather today was warm for the season, and the forecast for tomorrow was typical, she said, with the exception of the high wind, then asked what our plans were and how long we were staying. I said we were thinking about making our way over to Yellowstone, but our final destination was Oregon.

She admonished me to be very cautious tomorrow driving, then added, "I saw what you have. That's a nice big outfit. But if it was me, I would not go anywhere tomorrow!"

This was the second time someone remarked about the approaching sudden change in the weather accompanied by a high wind forecast for Wednesday. The first was the two guys I talked to earlier in the morning back in the town of Interior, while I was walking to the Post Office. I relayed the information to Todd.

He pondered this a bit, then said, "Maybe we should stay at this campground all day tomorrow. Part of our plan, which is why we got on I-90 instead of I-80, was to try to go through Yellowstone National Park. Now that we have discovered that a lot of stuff out here has closed in October for winter and the end of the tourist season, it seems this plan might be up in the air."

"You are absolutely right," I replied, then continued, "yet we are now positioned hundreds of miles north of where we should be in order to get to the Portland area. If we stay on I-90 we will end up in Seattle, Washington. Yellowstone was to be our path to get back on track back toward I-80. We are still over 1,200 miles from our destination. You got that message this afternoon from Amy, now telling us not to arrive before Monday because she had no place to park this thing. We have time to kill. We also have a long way to go!" No firm decision was made on any plan.

Nevertheless, there was still a strong sentiment that it would be neat to see Yellowstone.

In Ohio, the standing joke about the weather is that if you don't like it, wait five minutes because it will change. Conversely, if you do like the weather, enjoy every minute of it, because it will change. We had come to the understanding that out West the same may be true as well, but there could be grim consequences to taking a cavalier attitude about the weather here, especially with the approach of winter. The gates on the Interstate gave clear warning that winter is no joke and getting caught unaware could be a life and death mistake. A person or a vehicle may not be found for weeks, if not months. We took the warnings of the approaching cold front very seriously.

As a result of our long and late lunch, we did not bother with any supper. However, we did go outside to look at the night sky. The Big Dipper hung low in the Northwest and was very prominent. In the distance, we could hear industrial sounds that we figured might be coming from a sawmill. As our eyes adjusted to the dark, the Milky Way was faintly visible. Also, to the Northwest, lightning flashes could be seen illuminating big clouds. Some weather was brewing, and it appeared to be coming our way.

A little after 10 PM, the smoke alarm went off. I was not completely asleep, for a foul odor had disturbed my slumber. Now I was fully awake and out of bed. Flipping on a light, I saw that the living room and kitchen area was full of thick acrid smoke. I shut off the heater fans, which had been running on electric supplied by the park in order to save on propane. By this time Todd was up as well. We opened the doors and windows to ventilate the RV with the now cold night air. Then we tried to figure out what was burning, but we could not. Whatever it was, it did not seem to be burning now since the smoke was abating. There was no flame and no smoke on the outside of the RV. The smoke was only inside. Todd killed the batteries since we did not know whether they had been the source of the smoke and switched the furnace to propane. It took a few hours for most of the rank odor to leave, but the RV remained permeated with a smell like burnt plastic. Outside, it was the fresh scent of pine trees.

Chapter 7
Wind

Wednesday, October 3- Day 4

The excitement last night caused me to sleep late, to the ungodly hour of 6:30 AM. A shower and a change of clothes to rid myself of the bouquet of smoke was definitely needed. Although the RV was equipped with a shower, it was right beside the rear bedroom where Todd slept, so once I discovered that most RV parks had showers, I chose to use them and not wake my partner with my early morning rituals. Besides, I could take as long as I wanted, and not worry about using up all the hot water in the RV. The shower house at this park turned out to be a vast improvement over the one at Badlands. This one was heated, had real light fixtures, a nice floor, and was attractively decorated. Todd was up by the time I got back, and so was the sun. The sky was mostly clear, and the temperature was a balmy 68°. It appeared the thunderstorm seen last night had missed us. The Black Hills scenery from this location early in the morning was spectacular. I grabbed my camera and walked up to the main road to get some shots. A large rocky pine-covered ridge, towering over the valley we were in, was a little over a mile away and the sun illuminated the craggy stone cliffs perfectly.

Morning in the Black Hills of South Dakota, as viewed from the Whispering Pines RV Park. **Day 4**

Amy had sent Todd a text message inquiring as to when we would get to Portland, but he said he did not reply because he had been working on the furnace. The plastic fan fins we had not gotten out of the heat-exchanger had melted and burned up and was the cause of our smoke-out last night. I had no cell service, so I went back up to the road to get a weak signal and texted Amy back stating that due to the high wind advisory, chances were that we would stay in the Black Hills for the day, and said nothing about a projected arrival day. I also sent a text to Tammy telling her where we were and that there was no cellphone service – just weak signal for texts.

Meanwhile, Todd had found a NOAA weather radio station on the RV radio, which said the wind would arrive around 10 AM accompanied by rapidly falling temperatures. This was the only time we had found a NOAA radio signal during the whole trip, although we tried. He made the decision to hit the road and head west before the front hit, and maybe try to get around it with a couple hours of hard driving. I concurred with his plan, adding that if it got too bad we could pull over somewhere to wait it out.

Todd had checked the map, and it looked like at right turn out of Whispering Pines on to RT-385 would take us to I-90 near a town called Spearfish, a little over fifty miles northwest of Rapid City. This scenic route went by a huge rock formation called The Needles, and through Deadwood, South Dakota. However, a rustic directional sign located at the end of the RV park driveway, listing distance and direction to all the local wonders, indicated the way to I-90 was to go back through Rapid City. Figuring that the "locals" ought to know the better faster way, even though it meant backtracking, we turned left and followed the recommendation. The goal was to beat the approaching weather front, not see more natural splendor. It took over an hour to get back on I-90, so the scenic route may have been just as good timewise, but once we started it would have been too time-consuming to alter our course.

We had been on the Interstate for a little more than half an hour, and a few exits past Camper World, where we had fixed the furnace blower yesterday, when the wind hit. I could feel Todd fighting the wheel as the RV was buffeted by gusts.

Slate gray clouds signal a drastic change in the weather. I-90 west of Rapid City, South Dakota **Day 4**

"Whoa! This shit hit about two hours early!" I observed, then added, "So much for getting ahead of it!" As I looked over at Todd, all I could see out his side window was a stack of extension ladders about a foot away from the glass. A painting contractor's pickup truck was pulling a large utility trailer with ladder racks on its side, and was trying to pass us, but they were experiencing the same difficulty as Todd was, and fighting to stay in their own lane.

"I am backing off to let this moron pass before he hits me, or I hit him," Todd said, exasperated. "I have been watching him come up the passing lane, weaving back and forth every time the wind hits him, and he has just about taken out every vehicle he has passed. Hell, I am doing almost 70 miles an hour!"

"Does this thing handle any better if you slow down?" I asked.

"Not really," he replied, "the wind is hitting at an angle from the right, so it is catching our side. It doesn't seem to matter what speed we go because it just slams you."

Low dark clouds were hugging the tops of the hills in the distance. The clear calm sunny morning was no more. An overhead traffic advisory sign stated, "High Wind Alert – Wind Gusts 48 mph – High Profile Vehicles Use Caution."

Todd drove a little while longer until we hit the Wyoming state line a couple of miles west of Spearfish, South Dakota, and we got off at Exit 205 for the Welcome Center. The exit ramp had cattle grates in it to prevent animals from wandering up on the Interstate. The road at the end of the ramp was like a county or township road, in that it was narrow and crudely paved. A small handmade sign pointed north to Devils Tower – 35 miles. Other than the travel center on the side of a hill, there was not much else. To the north was a two-lane road that paralleled the main road. Gates were at the ends of the ramps, and up on the Interstate, in order to close the road to all access in the event of bad weather. Not being sure if the high wind and dropping temperature we were encountering, or whatever else was coming, would be considered bad weather out here, we did not want to find ourselves stranded in a more remote location than this. Todd suggested we might have to park at the welcome center for a while, since at least they had restrooms and a large lot. The temperature had dropped to the low 50s, an almost twenty-degree plunge in about two hours.

Low clouds & high wind, I-90 near Spearfish, SD.

Mountain lion sculpture, I-90 Wyoming Welcome Center Where we stopped for weather conditions ahead. **Day 4**

The building was fairly new and modern, yet had a rustic appearance due to the stone and timber construction. A woman standing at a workstation in the lobby was looking at three computer monitors and assisting a couple of other travelers. I wandered around looking at the displays. Most impressive was the stuffed grizzly bear rearing up on his hind legs. I concluded that I really did not want to encounter something like him out in the wild, or anywhere else where we would be face to face. I also located a stack of Wyoming maps, which looked quite good, and free coffee. All the while I was eavesdropping on the conversations the lady was having with other travelers who had questions regarding access to Devils Tower and Yellowstone, as well as road conditions farther west, none of which sounded very encouraging. It was snowing at Devils Tower, and the road was bad, so we were definitely not taking a detour to see that natural wonder today, especially not in an RV.

The fastest route toward Yellowstone was to take I-90 west for about 180 miles to just past Sheridan, Wyoming, and then get off on US-14 and head southwest toward Cody. Unfortunately, fog and snow were being reported around Sheridan, and the mountain passes were definitely getting snow. She recommended getting off at Buffalo, a distance of a little over 100 miles, and then take US-16 over the passes, before zigzagging over to Cody. There were not any other road choices. Snow was now the determining factor for advisable routes. The other point she stressed was that right now all roads were open, as were the parks, but with an early winter storm like this there was no telling how long that would remain the case, and once the roads through some of the passes closed, they stayed closed for the rest of winter. Welcome to Wyoming, indeed!

I thought again about people in Ohio who complain about the weather because of the extremes, and that it changes so frequently. But we do not have to face decisions like the closure of roads for months. This was definitely adding a bit more excitement to the trip.

I relayed the information to Todd, who responded, "Well, I guess we are going to Buffalo then!"

"I will take over driving. You have had your fun with the wind for several hours. Now it is my turn!"

"Be my guest, bubba!" Todd said grinning.

The trip on I-90 through Wyoming was quite interesting. First, there was the challenge of keeping the RV in the proper lane, and when crossing large gullies and valleys we would be hit with strong crosswinds. It was tricky work, but I did okay. The other interesting thing was the continual change in the landscape. We went from large rolling hills covered with pine trees to vast rolling scrubland, and then the oil, gas, and coal lands. The hamlet of Sundance was home to the 1890 era gunslinger The Sundance Kid, or at least that is what a big sign proclaimed. The Burlington Northern Santa Fe (BNSF) Railroad ran nearby for much of the drive, so we got to see unit trains of coal hoppers or oil tankers, as well as the returning empties. Three or four engines would be pulling, and two engines would be pushing from the rear in order to get the two-mile-long trains over the grades. For a railroad fan like myself, I thoroughly enjoyed the show. Todd was more curious about how I knew all this weird stuff.

Gillette, Wyoming had been a sleepy high plains Western town until oil, gas, and low- Sulphur coal was discovered in the Powder River Basin about twenty or thirty years ago. Now it was an energy boomtown. The existence of the coal in the area had been known for over one hundred years, but it had been considered to be of lower quality compared to coal extracted from the Appalachian Mountains, which burned easier and hotter. Determining that this Powder River Basin coal produced less pollution when burned changed that whole equation. Western coal became more desirable for power generating purposes. Now the town had spread to both sides of the Interstate in a wide bowl. A coal processing and train loading facility dominated the valley, at least until we went by a huge open-pit coal strip mine which was eating a gigantic hole into the mountain to the north. Beat up mobile homes and shabby little one-story houses packed the sides of the adjacent roads, interspersed by various industrial service companies. The Interstate crossed a new looking five-lane street, lined with fast-food restaurants, car lots, and mineral extraction businesses. This appeared to be what served as the business district, for there was no distinct or obvious downtown. Other than the coal processing structure, everything else had a temporary or impermanent appearance to it. On a ridge to the west were some nicer homes and business buildings, but not many. The edge of the scrub grassland was visible surrounding the whole area, and yet a large part of the energy resources for the United States of America was emanating from this scruffy place. It was fascinating to see, and I knew we were only viewing a part of the total extent of the mining and extraction lands. Gillette just happens to be at the center of it all.

When we finally got off the Interstate and drove into the town of Buffalo, the cloud cover had thickened, and the air was damp. The wind had not abated. We figured we ought to fuel the RV and get some extra coolant. Todd had noticed the coolant overflow tank had lost a couple of quarts the past two days. We also needed a couple more of jugs of water for us, since the RV tap water was undrinkable, and lunch seemed like a good idea as well. The RV got taken care of, and I got several jugs of water for the fridge. By all appearances, Buffalo seemed to be a thriving place, and we assumed there would be a restaurant on down the road, but we saw none. Within a couple of minutes, the two-lane pavement of US-16 had by-passed the old business district and left town and was climbing up tree-covered hills. Ironically, US-16, along with state route 385, ran in front of the campground where we stayed the previous night in the Black Hills. It would have been a scenic drive from the campground to Buffalo, but we would still have been in South Dakota if we had taken that route instead of the Interstate.

In very short order we encountered fog, then rain, and then the rain changed to snow. Fortunately, it was not sticking, but snow was definitely falling. It looked rather pretty swirling through the pine trees and fog. We did see an elevation marker as we drove through a pass, "Powder River Pass elevation 9,665 feet", but with the fog and blowing snow, all we could see was pine trees and big rocks. Only later, when looking at the map, did we realize we had just crossed the Bighorn Mountains, and there was a mountain named Hazelton Peak, with a height of 10,535 feet, just about a mile away. We could not see any of it, nor did we have a clue where we were!

US-16 out of Buffalo, Wyoming, climbing into fog, rain, then snow, at Powder River Pass. **Day 4**

Near the summit of Powder River Pass, peaks in the clouds, snow markers along the road. Elevation 9,665 feet, in the Big Horn Mountains of Wyoming. **Day 4**

West side of the Big Horn Mountains, after crossing Powder River Pass. A dramatic change of scenery and weather. US-16 in Wyoming. **Day 4**

Ten Sleep Canyon, leading us out of the Big Horn Mountains, on US-16 in Wyoming. **Day 4**

The road went along a somewhat level area, and the snow stopped, and it now seemed like we were in the clouds. As the road began its descent the clouds dissipated and there were high clouds and some sun. We could see we were going down through a large crevasse, named Ten Sleep Canyon. Rock walls rose over a thousand feet on either side. Occasionally we could catch a glimpse of a rock-filled stream at the bottom of the canyon. I was glad Todd was driving, for that allowed me to take some pictures, and really gawk at the stunning scenery from the windows on either side of the motorhome. After a while, the road and the stream were at the same level, for we had reached the bottom and the mouth of the canyon. The canyon opened up to a scrub grass plateau. Trees lined the stream, and we spotted several fly fishermen trying their luck. Crossing a small bridge, the sign stated this was Ten Sleep Creek. Fences appeared, and then a scattering of houses, and finally the town of Ten Sleep, Wyoming. This little berg was very attractive, nicely kept houses and buildings, and the streets were well paved, and even had curbs and sidewalks. The residents had landscaping and shrubbery, instead of beat-up vehicles on blocks, or partial carcasses of snowmobiles decorating their yards, like we had seen in some other places along the way. There were three or four restaurants, but no place to park a huge RV. The town had half a dozen cross streets which all appeared to vanish into the scrub. No lunch here, which was a shame, for it was a very appealing place, and we were really hungry.

Rolling scrub land, west of Ten Sleep, Wyoming. All alone on US-16 heading generally west **Day 4**

The next town was called Worland, and it was twenty-six miles away, so we pressed on. This place was sizable enough to have a couple of fast-food joints, and even a couple of motels. Our route changed from mostly west to almost due north. Worland had some nice old turn of the century two and three-story brick and stone buildings downtown. One block to the west was a railroad, several old grain elevators, a small rail yard, but alas, no obvious or convenient place to park this rig.

Old hotel in Worland, Wyoming. Back in civilization, but no place to park the RV to get lunch. US-16 / US-20 / RT-789 heading north along the Big Horn River, with an arm of the Big Horn Mountains visible in the distance more than twenty miles away. **Day 4**

"Anything else on this road?" Todd asked as we rolled north out of town.
"There is small town about twenty miles up the road, and then a bigger town another eleven miles on past that. It's called Basin, and that might be our best bet. After that is a town called Greybull, where we change direction and head west toward Cody," I said, while checking the Rand McNally Road Atlas.

"Can we make it to Cody today, in daylight?" Todd queried.

"Should not be a problem. Cody appears to be a little over one hundred miles away."

The state of Wyoming has relatively few paved roads and a lot of distance to cover. Fortunately, those roads are usually very nice, in that they are well paved and have decent berms on the sides and can accommodate a bus like we were driving rather well. Often, whatever road we were on was actually a combined route, so this road heading north out of Worland was US-16 / US-20 and state RT-789. As it turned out, over the next several days we would find ourselves on a couple of these same routes, only in other parts of the state. The small side roads were either gravel or graded packed dirt.

We were on the eastern edge of a broad basin, appropriately called The Big Horn Basin, with the road on the east bank of the Bighorn River. Ten to twenty miles to the east were the foothills of the Bighorn Mountains, which we had crossed over hours before in snow and fog. Straight ahead we could see more of the Bighorn Range transecting our path in the distance. Across the river to the west was most of the basin, with some irrigated hay fields. Occasionally, far to the west we could glimpse the faint hazy outline of another mountain range, which turned out to be the Rocky Mountains. Between the road and the river ran the tracks of the Burlington Northern Santa Fe (BNSF) Railroad.

Hay appeared to be the major agricultural commodity. Farms were crude affairs, not the major building complexes we were used to seeing in Ohio, with neat, fenced fields and several crops. Actually, most of the scattered houses were similar to what was observed in South Dakota, meaning ragged looking modular houses, with homemade additions, abandoned cars, trucks, trailers, appliances, and snow mobiles strewn about the property, one or two small low barns, and a huge stack of jumbo-size hay bales to feed unseen livestock through the long winter months. In a way, it looked like Appalachia in eastern and southeastern Ohio, with the exception of the giant hay bales and snowmobile carcasses, replacing the dense vegetation and steep hills and hollows with flatness, scrub grass, and sage brush. There would also be a cluster of low trees around these visions of human chaos. How any of this provided an income, let alone a living wage, was a total mystery. The always present scattering of vehicles made it hard to tell which one was the primary mode of transportation, and which ones died where they sat. Rarely were any people visible, but if they were, they were men near an open barn door, or near a pickup truck or trailer, and what activity was being conducted remained obscure. It was the familiar look of a mean life and poverty, where you do not get rid of anything because it might prove useful later or cost too much to haul away. Any cost is too much when living hand to mouth, day to day. Having lived that way during my drinking years, I understood the mindset, for to some extent it is still with me today and is also recognizable from my years working at the foodbank serving these very same types of folks.

There was no sign stating the name of the town, but humanity had clustered along both sides of the road, in the form of numerous structures. Elsewhere in Wyoming there would have been an incongruous sign proudly declaring the location, and a population barely in double digits. But not this place. To call it a town would have been too generous a term anyway. It was more like the same odd rural homesteads viewed near and far from the road had all congealed into close proximity for a quarter mile or so. There were apparently some vehicle repair shops, but those were largely inferred due to the bigger size of the rusty metal buildings and an increase in the number of vehicle parts and pieces strewn about, plus several primitive signs stating the obvious, 'repairs.' Even these properties, in this so-called town, had the ubiquitous big stack of hay somewhere on the premises, to feed the invisible livestock. Lunch, a cup of coffee, or fuel, was not even a remote possibility here.

As Todd looked out at the corroded scene, he affected the voice of a prideful man, "Yup! Got the first car I ever had! Ah, '68 Chevy Biscayne! Right over there! And I got all my other ones too!"

"Don't forget your pick'em up trucks, and yer snowmobiles!"

"Yup, got them too!" Todd retorted, with a big inhale of satisfaction.

"You a rich man!" I replied with sincere admiration.

The mountains to the north and east had gotten close enough that the road and the railroad were forced to cross over to the west bank of the Bighorn River. This change took place near a largely unseen town called Manderson, which was somewhere in a cluster of trees. The next town, named Basin, appeared to have been prosperous many decades ago. There were a couple of old grain elevators along the railroad, and the streets were wide and smoothly paved. More importantly, there was a restaurant on the main street, which actually appeared to be open as we rolled past, so Todd went around the block and parked the RV on a side street. We walked half a block to the illuminated "OPEN" sign. That, and the grease ventilator on the roof, were the only tip-offs that food was served inside the low single-story building of cinder block and weathered plywood because there was no other discernible sign stating the purpose of this place. The name could have been the Wagon Wheel, or some such western theme name, but once inside we learned it was called the Black Mountain Grill, which was even better. It was 3:30 PM, and this late lunch was our first real stop since morning at the rest area on I-90. We had driven hundreds of miles under trying conditions and spectacular scenery—when we could actually see. The weather had run the gamut. Clear morning, strong wind, more wind, fog, in clouds, rain and snow, and now hazy sun with the temperature cool and in the low 50s. It was refreshing to take a brief walk and sit down in a chair that was not moving.

  The waitress was friendly, which made this respite more enjoyable. Unfortunately, my food got stuck in my esophagus on about the third bite, so I stared at the television while I waited for the dry fish to finally go down. Todd inhaled his lunch, in his typical fashion, and then took note there was no progress being made on my plate.

"I'm going to ask them to turn off the TV if you don't start eating your meal!"

I briefly explained the medical issue—lack of esophageal movement.

"Want me to do the hammock on ya?"

"It's called the Heimlich Maneuver! And, no, that does not help. The food is stuck in my swaller pipe, not my windpipe!" I replied, trying to make light of an embarrassing and potentially lengthy situation. It was taking so long for the blockage to resume its downward path that I offered the rest of my meal to Todd, and he readily accepted. This condition happens somewhat frequently to me, and I had hoped it would not happen on this trip so that I would not have to explain it or embarrass myself by choking and regurgitating at a dinner table. To think I would be immune from this occurring was not realistic, but I had my hopes. Now another secret was out. By the time the food had dislodged itself, and I had paid for the three-bite meal, Todd had left and gotten the RV and was waiting outside the restaurant ready to roll.

Greybull was the next town up the Bighorn River, and where we would change direction and head west on US-16/US-20, plus US-14 toward Cody, a little over fifty miles away. This is where we would have been had we been able to cross over the Big Horn Mountains west of Sheridan, and not taken the route we did due to snow in that pass. Some of the land was rolling, and some flat, and all was sparsely covered by low scrub brush. Along one of the flat stretches was the hamlet of Emblem, Wyoming – population 15. It consisted of maybe half a dozen old homes, four of which appeared to be almost habitable, in a clump of rangy gnarled trees, but it did rate its own tiny US Post Office, which was about the size of a yard shed.

Shadowy forms of mountains appeared, then disappeared, only to reappear closer and larger after we emerged from another gully or climbed over a low hill. These were definitely the Rocky Mountains, and Cody was somewhere near the base of them. The map indicated some of the peaks were over 12,000 feet and were impressive considering how far away they still were.

Empty road west of Greybull, Wyoming. Silhouette of the Rocky Mountains 50 miles in the distance. **Day 4**

The mountains kept getting closer, and finally, the front-range became more distinct, which then obscured the higher mountains we had been looking at for over an hour. The road was clearly heading toward a gap in the mountains. Out near Yellowstone Regional Airport, on the east fringe of town, we passed the KOA Campground, and it was closed. Then, with no transition, the trees and businesses of Cody suddenly materialized and the road descended into town.

A treaty signed in 1868 between the local Native American tribes and the Federal Government put the whole Big Horn Basin in Native hands, and off-limits to white settlers. Ten years later the treaty was broken, and white settlers began to come into the basin. This made the area one of the last frontiers settled in the lower 48 states.

William F. "Buffalo Bill" Cody was visiting Sheridan, Wyoming in 1894 when his son-in-law, Horace Boal, took him to the top of the Big Horn Mountains to have a view looking out toward the northwestern part of the basin. Although Cody had heard of this area from Indians, he had never personally been to the northern basin. Upon learning that a group of Sheridan businessmen were interested in establishing a town in the northwestern part of the basin, Cody joined in the effort. He saw beauty in the region, and its proximity to Yellowstone was already attracting tourists.

Water for the proposed town was a necessity, so in the fall of 1895 construction on the Cody canal was begun to carry water from the South Fork of the Shoshone River toward the probable location of the town. This would provide irrigation water to the area and drinking water to the town as well. George T. Beck, Cody's Wild West partner, and a few other businessmen of means, created a land and irrigation company to establish the town, which was surveyed in 1896. "The Colonel," as the townspeople often referred to "Buffalo Bill," invested a great deal of money in the construction of the town, which would be named in his honor. By 1900, the fledgling town had a population of 300. The Chicago, Burlington & Quincy Railroad built a rail spur from Toluca, Montana to Cody, Wyoming, which opened in 1901. In 1902 a hotel, named The Irma, for Cody's daughter, opened and proclaimed it was the most modern hotel in the Rockies.

Oil was discovered in the Oregon Basin southeast of the town, which spurred additional growth. The Husky Oil Company moved their headquarters to town and built a refinery. Husky was sold, and the refinery was closed in the mid-1980s, but Marathon Oil established a regional headquarters in the former Husky building and continues its presence today.

Currently there are approximately 9,500 year-round residents in Cody, but the population swells during tourist season, and for the Cody Stampede Rodeo, which runs every night during the same season. The primary businesses are oil and gas, agriculture, tourism, and service industries. We were informed later that we missed the rodeo experience by three days, since it concludes its season at the end of September.

The main drag of Cody was several blocks long and lined with interesting stone and brick buildings from the late 1890s to early 1900s. Downtown looked substantial and permanent, which was nice. It was evening rush hour in Cody, and the traffic crept from block to block at each traffic light, which allowed us to really look the place over. This took about ten minutes. On the west side of town, we spotted an RV park called The Ponderosa.

Gap in mountains near Cody, Wyoming—plus, trees reappear.
Day 4

Downtown Cody, Wyoming during evening rush hour. Very tolerable traffic.

It was a convenient and scenic location; even better given the fact it was the only RV park open. A two-story log office, which looked like a large lodge, with a wraparound covered porch, fronted the main street. The entrance drive went between the log building and another building that contained shower facilities, a laundromat, game room, and other amenities. The log office also had a souvenir and outdoor supply store, plus a minimal convenient store. Large tall trees lined the drive to the camper parking area.

We both looked around, and Todd remarked, "Man, this looks really nice! Better not cost too much, especially since there is no other option! We are going to have to pay whatever they ask!"

"Too bad we are not wearing jangling spurs on our boots, so we could sound really authentic walking up these wooden steps," I joked as we headed for the office. Two women eyed us from chairs behind a glass showcase containing knives, feathers, and other western style trinkets. Racks of tourist pamphlets were to either side, and the rest of the large rustic room contained coats, sweatshirts, and weird little tourist knick-knacks for sale.

Todd walked up to the counter while I fingered through the pamphlets.

"Can I help you?" the younger woman, who appeared to be around sixty, asked as she stood up. The older woman, probably in her late seventies, eyed us skeptically while remaining seated with a Styrofoam coffee cup in her hand.

"Yeah, you certainly can," Todd replied, "We need a space for an RV, preferably with all hook-ups."

"What size motor home?" she asked.

"A thirty-seven-foot Southwind with three sliders," Todd responded.

"Oh, a big one!" the woman retorted, "I have a space for it, and it should be fairly easy to get into."

"I like the sound of that," Todd said.

"So, is it two couples?" she cheerily asked, while getting paperwork from the other woman, who was now on her feet.

"We are the couple!" I interjected, "But not like you think! Even though you may have had couples like that, we are not! In fact, we are not even sure we like each other!"

"You will fit in just fine here!" the younger woman chuckled. The older woman pursed her lips and narrowed her gaze at both of us.

Entrance to the Ponderosa RV Park, Cody WY **Day 4**

View of the mountain west of Cody, from our Ponderosa RV Park site.

Our spot was very convenient to get into, as promised, and had all hookups. Another bonus was it was not a far walk from the only shower house still open, which was up by the office. The rest of the showers and laundries had been shut down for the winter. We also had a fairly good view of the mountains just a few miles to the west, and the gap going through them. Todd got the water line and sewer line connected while I plugged in the electric and the cable TV. He seemed very excited about the prospect of watching television tonight. I got my camera and walked to the edge of a ravine by the park to look at the scenery. Meanwhile, Todd went back to the office to inquire about rental cars and was told to "talk to Larry" in the morning. We had discussed the practicality of renting a car to drive around in Yellowstone, rather than taking the RV, which seemed like a fine idea. There were three car rental companies, all located back at the airport, according to his computer. At 6 PM, none of them were answering their phone, much to Todd's chagrin.

"Maybe they are closed for the season!" I opined. Todd shook his head in disgust.

The cable TV provided a weather update and stated there was a high probability of rain showers tomorrow. The local channels were from Montana, and early in the evening they consisted of a little bit of news plus a constant barrage of political ads by candidates for various offices and state ballot issues. Most of the ads sounded like they were narrated by the same sinister deep-voiced man. After twenty minutes of this onslaught, one was left with the impression that all the candidates were nothing short of egg-sucking dogs, and all the ballot issues would bankrupt the state. Todd switched to a couple of 'reality' shows, which were not much of an improvement. I found writing in my journal was much more stimulating. Todd found my company wanting and retired to the back bedroom to watch TV in peace.

Chapter 8
Yellowstone

Thursday, October 4- Day 5

I got up a little before 5 AM, packed up the hide-a-bed, and headed over to the laundry and shower building in a steady light rain. The temperature was 37° according to the illuminated welcome sign by the park office. My clothes needed to have the smell of plastic smoke and RV funk washed out, so I was glad this park had the facilities to do that. Before taking a shower, I gave Tammy a call while standing outside and smoking a cigarette. I told her of our plan to go to Yellowstone National Park today, rain or no rain. She was once again less than thrilled about me possibly getting to see all this natural wonder without her. This is what we were supposed to do together, and that was my dream as well, so I fully sympathized with her disappointment, but I was here now and planned to take full advantage of it.

Mercifully, the shower room was heated. It had about five showers, a couple of sinks, and several toilet stalls. I was more impressed by this operation all the time. The clothes were done drying by the time I had finished with the shower and shave. Another early riser came into the laundry while I was folding my clothes. She was from California and was on a grand tour of the United States with another family. They had a total of seven kids, and a dog, all packed into a small camper RV. I told her I could not imagine that many people in the huge RV Todd and I were in, let alone in a really small one.

"After a couple of days of that, people would start to come up missing!" I mused.

"Oh, we all get along," she stated with grim certainty.

"So where to next?" I asked.

"We're headed for Niagara Falls, and stopping in Chicago along the way. Then visiting friends in Cincinnati on the way back. We did Yellowstone yesterday," she declared.

"You could not find someplace else nearby to visit?" I asked.

"We have three weeks to do it, and we figured this was our only chance to do this. So yeah, see it all if we can," she replied, full of optimism.

"Niagara Falls is great. My wife and I were there about two years ago. I think your kids will be impressed. And while you are in Ohio, take the time to make a detour into the southeastern portion of the state to visit the Hocking Hills area. There are a number of state parks, with relatively short hikes to scenic cliffs and waterfalls. It will be worth the time, especially since you are trying to see it all. Good luck on your trip!" I said as I headed for the door.

Todd was up by the time I got back, so after a cup of coffee, we headed over to the office to talk to Larry about getting a rental car. He was a character, which must be a requirement for people who run RV parks. Larry connected us to one of the car rental places out at the airport and informed us that two of them were run by the same people. He also cautioned us about traveling in Yellowstone.

"Watch out for the animals! You are in their home, and they do not pay much attention to cars, and they consider any of the roads to be theirs! But the real problem is the tourists slamming on their brakes to stop and look at animals wherever they are. And another thing, there has been major road construction up there all year, so you might run into that as well. Although it is getting rather late in the season for them to be working, but all summer it was a mess!" Larry advised. We thanked him for the info. I mailed postcards to Tammy and my mom, while Todd examined the merchandise. I went outside for a smoke but did not even have time to fire one up before a girl driving a Hyundai whipped into a parking spot out front and gave me a long look.

"Rental car?" I asked.

"Yes. You Todd Brady?" she asked.

"No, I am with him, and I will go fetch him," I replied.

We got into the car for the drive back to the airport to take care of the paperwork. The young lady veered off onto a side street, then zigzagged through a nice newer looking residential neighborhood of ranch and split-level houses up on a hill, before coming out on a highway somewhere.

"What is the name of this road?" I inquired.

"I don't know! I have only lived here a little over a year!" she cheerfully replied.

"Well, I'm lost! We have only been here a little over twelve hours, and we were asleep during most of that," I said while trying to find a familiar landmark. Soon we were almost out of town when she made a turn into the airport.

"Thank God I was paying attention when we arrived last evening," I thought to myself. "At least I know approximately where we are and can get us back to the RV."

That is exactly what we did, along with a quick stop at a Walgreens drug store to pick up more film for my camera, and shampoo for Todd. We grabbed our stuff out of the RV and then headed to a nondescript restaurant for breakfast, where the 'locals' ate, according to Larry at the RV park. We were on the road west toward Yellowstone by 10:30 AM. US-16 / US-20 went through the gap we had looked at the night before as we approached town and could view from our campsite. Buffalo Bill Dam was at the bottom of the canyon in the gap, and down out of sight from the road. Completed in 1910, the dam is 325 feet tall, concrete arch construction, and was the highest dam in the world at the time of its completion. The road went through two short tunnels, and then a very long one blasted through impressive looking rock. Upon exiting the long tunnel, we were greeted by a view of the waters of Buffalo Bill Lake, surrounded by mountains. The entrance to Yellowstone Park was a little over fifty miles away.

Since I was driving, I chose to stop wherever something looked interesting. First, I pulled off to look at the lake, and then a stop along the river we were following upstream. It turned out to be North Fork of the Shoshone River, and we were following it toward the larger mountains and the park. This was a very scenic drive, and since the rain had stopped several hours earlier the visibility was good. Periodically the sun briefly broke through and shone on the yellow autumn leaves of box elder trees along the river. The effect was spectacular, but hard to get a decent looking photo of because the sun mostly stayed behind the clouds.

Interest in photography runs in my family. My grandfather, Fred Way Jr., was a river boat captain on the Ohio River, and steamboat historian, as well as a photographer and writer, who taught my dad when he was young, how to develop photographic film and print black and white photos, and gave him some instruction on taking pictures. Dad had a darkroom in the basement of the house where I grew up, and he taught my brother and me the processes he had learned. I have been taking pictures since I was about twelve years old. Over the years I have tried to improve my photographic techniques, and my camera equipment, but most of the time I simply record what I encounter. For this trip, I brought over a dozen rolls of film and figured I would shoot a lot in Yellowstone, which is why I added to the film stash I already had. If time and lighting permitted the creation of artistically pleasing shots, then so much the better, but I figured that most of the fast shooting I would be doing would just be snapshots of the journey. Todd questioned why I still used film instead of switching to digital, which is a query I often receive. Simply put, I prefer the permanence of film and prints, as well as the results. Digital technology is changing so fast that it becomes too expensive for me to keep upgrading, and the image storage and retrieval platforms will be outdated well before my 'old-school' photos fade away. That said, I brought Tammy's old smartphone so I could use it in low light situations or if my camera got damaged by exposure to the elements. That is my well-rehearsed explanation for holding on to ancient technology as long as I can. Old cameras feel comfortable, and I do not really mind sending the film out for processing and printing and waiting in anticipation to see if I actually took some good pictures, or sacrificed time, money, and film for unremarkable results. One learns patience and accepts disappointment. I find the photographic act to be calming, yet exhilarating, and satiates much of my creative yearnings.

North Fork Valley, looking back toward Cody. Getting the last hay cutting before winter. **Day 5**

Low clouds obscuring the distant, and much larger, mountains beyond a green hayfield in the North Fork Valley on the way to Yellowstone National Park. **Day 5**

    The park pass I bought back at the Badlands got us into Yellowstone National Park for free, which was an unexpected bonus. The road, once in the park, was much narrower than the road in the valley due to the close proximity of cliffs and mountainsides, some of which reached a height of over 10,000 feet. Soon the road became twisty and curvy while climbing up through steep valleys. The clouds got lower and it began to rain. We had been in Shoshone Canyon even before entering the park, and now it was climbing steeply into the mountains. The road topped out at Sylvan Pass, elevation 8,559 feet, but we could see little except for rock walls and some close by pine trees, due to the mist and low clouds. Nevertheless, it was still impressive.

    The road made a hairpin turn, then began climbing sharply again along the side of a very deep ravine. There was a pull-off, so that is what I did, not wanting to miss anything. Oddly, there was no stream at the bottom of this gouge in the mountainside, but down below it joined the canyon we had just come out of. We were surprised to find hillsides were comprised of boulders and stones instead of solid rock. On the north-facing mountain across the other side of the canyon there were two patches of white. Todd checked them out with his binoculars and stated it was ice. The whole area appeared to us to be ripe for a massive landslide, especially with the rain, so we jumped back in the car and took off again.

Road construction season had just ended, and the work ceased at whatever point in the job they got to, which in the first encounter was no pavement, just gravel, potholes, and a very wide graded right-of-way. The road equipment was parked in the woods for the winter. The Hyundai Elantra rental car handled the rough road rather well, and I could have gone faster but traffic ahead would not permit that. During the rest of our travels in the park, we encountered a couple more of these long road construction zones, each a mile or more in length.

The size of Yellowstone Lake caught us by surprise, even though I was vaguely aware that a small steamship had operated on the lake in the 1890s. The opposite shore was miles away, and for a time not visible due to the distance across and the smoky spume blowing off the wind-whipped waves. Waves smashed against the wall that the road was above, and the spray was blowing across the pavement in sheets. In other places there were hot springs at the edge of the lake and clouds of vapor, smelling like sulphur, blew across the road. The further we drove the more excited we got, for we were now seeing truly strange and new sights.

Just past Fishing Bridge we came to a crossroad and took the one heading north toward the interior of the park, and the promise of seeing real volcanic action. Mud Volcano was the first encounter. Hot springs boiled out of the side of a hill, right in front of the parking area. We got out of the car and headed through the light rain toward the steam rising out of the earth. Wooden boardwalks provided close access to several of the features, and the walks were crammed with scores of Japanese tourists. It was fascinating to watch both the tourists and the bubbling burping mud. We stopped at a couple of other features, and the further we drove the more hot springs could be seen off in the distance all over the area. Clouds of steam rising out of the trees, or along streams, or out in meadows, indicated their presence and prevalence. The soil around the steam vents was usually white, but there were other colors like light green and rust red. Brilliant green grasses and algae rimming a lot of the vents, but only for about six inches along the perimeter, and then it would be scrub brush or more mud. The mud vents were typically cement gray, with a consistency of hot fudge. Hissing was heard anywhere near the vents.

Burping vent near Mud Volcano.

Other vents in the area. Sulphur Caldron. **Day 5**

Volcanic mist rising to meet low clouds, in the valley beyond burnt trees from a forest fire years ago. The very large mountains in the distance are mostly obscured by the clouds.
Yellowstone National Park

Yellowstone   *Bright green grasses at the edge of a boiling mud vent.*   **Day 5**

Grand Canyon of The Yellowstone, below the Lower Falls, cut through ancient yellow volcanic gravel, over 1,000 feet deep, and the first sight from Artist Point.

Lower Falls of the Yellowstone River viewed from Artist Point. The river falls 308 feet, higher than Niagara Falls.

Lower Falls of the Yellowstone River, at Artist Point. Yellowstone Canyon below the Lower Falls.

    We continued our northerly course, taking in the varying views from the road. Evidence of the huge forest fire in 1988, or maybe other ones since then, was visible throughout the park. The undergrowth was green, but the blackened spires of torched pine trees covered large swaths of area, yet equally large areas had been completely untouched by flames. Due to the vigorous undergrowth, it was plain that the fires occurred some years back, yet the contrast between the burnt and the spared forest remained quite stark. The rain came and went, as did the fog and low clouds, so visibility varied greatly mile by mile, or mountain ridge to mountain ridge.

    Signs pointed toward a lodge and restaurant at a location called Tower-Roosevelt. We were hungry, but one glimpse of the crowded parking lot meant it would be a long wait for a meal, so on we drove. An old, weathered cement block gas station suddenly materialized along the side of the forested road. It looked completely out of place after hours of driving through amazing natural landscape. Nevertheless, the prospect of overpriced convenience food and a quick break was too much to resist. The crude building did not portend a shiny oasis, but it did have gasoline, offered minor repairs and towing, plus hot fluid vaguely resembling coffee, and a slim selection of candy. This was a rescue business, not a noted tourist stop. I went for coffee and a couple of giant Milky Way bars, then headed outside for a smoke. I wanted to soak up the aroma of the pine forest and contemplate upon the sheer wonder of just being where I was. Todd wandered out of the station, carrying something, and declared that he would take over driving. Had I known what the ride would be like for the next half hour or so, I might have protested.

To say my traveling partner is an aggressive driver is stating the fact a bit mildly. My style is smooth and defensive, as instilled into me by my parents. However, I drive a lot faster than either of them would be comfortable with, but only when I feel it is safe, which is not to be confused with being legal. Todd, however, prefers fast starts and passing anything that is in front of him whenever possible, along with a non-stop profane commentary of the poor operational skills of those sharing the same pavement. This is not to say he is unsafe, for he truly is a professional driver, but for a person like me, his driving style takes a bit of getting used to, especially when he fiddled with his phone to make calls, text, try to look at a map or select music on his iPod.

Todd's choice of a snack to eat proved most unfortunate for my nerves. The road became even twistier than before and exited the comforting confines of forest in close proximity, to a landscape of deep ravines and majestic valleys of rock and grass. The narrow pavement had no berm, no guard rail or cables, and even lacked the decency of painted lines. The edge simply vanished to the bottom thousands of feet below. While navigating this, and wanting to pass other vehicles, Todd was also trying to unwrap the tin foil off Hershey's Chocolate Kisses, which meant he had to drive with his wrists and look at the candy instead of the road. In some areas, the clouds were breaking up so the expansive views of the valleys and canyons was extraordinary, but I was having a difficult time appreciating it for fear we would soon leave the road for an up-close and personal look at the bottom. I was praying he had purchased a small bag of Kisses, but it appeared to be bottomless, so I tried to focus on the distant views and ignore what was going on in the driver's seat next to me. Then I would hear the plastic bag rustle again as he reached for another. It was truly terrifying, and the crinkling of the bag meant the excruciation would continue a bit longer.

A high valley, viewed during the terrifying Chocolate Kisses distracted drive. **Yellowstone National Park.**

A small portion of Mammoth Hot Springs. Yellowstone National Park

This went on until we reached Mammoth Hot Springs, although we did stop briefly at Undine Falls to check that out. Pretty view, however, after seeing the Lower Falls of the Yellowstone, this was not even in the same league. An Asian girl stopped me on my way back from the overlook and asked, basically, if it was worth the effort to go see it. I told her since she only had about two hundred feet to go, she may as well trudge on and enjoy the view. She smiled and thanked me profusely.

Mammoth Hot Springs turned out to be not only as the name implied, but also an old fort, a village, an old plain wood hotel that was being restored, a newer lodge, and lots of parking lots. We did not stop since Todd had wanted to pass a line of slow-moving cars for the past several miles and hoped most would pull off at this place. Fortunately, most of them did, which only left the lead car still crawling along, and as it turned out, this one was sporting Florida tags. This was too much! Todd floored the Hyundai rental to pass just as the offending car pulled into the final parking lot. The springs themselves were extensive, impressive, and truly mammoth. Terraces of white salts cascaded down from the hillside, with steam rising from the whole mass. Boardwalks zig-zagged out of the parking lots, across vaporous mudflats and up the hillside. Curious white solid formations, similar to cavern stalactites, flowed down the edges of the terraces to the next level. It would have been easy to spend a couple of hours just at this location, because of the sheer size of the formations, and how spectacular they were, but we now had an appointment to see Old Faithful, and nothing was going to get in our way—wildlife and sightseers be damned!

The road headed south from Mammoth Hot Springs and began a winding ascent to another pass. Fortunately, Todd had finished his bag of Hershey's

Kisses and could focus solely on driving like a madman. He suddenly whipped across the road to a turnout in a narrow deep canyon, just as a double tanker gasoline truck appeared at the crest of the curvy road up ahead. According to the signs, this location is called Golden Gate, and the artist Thomas Moran created a famous painting of this canyon in 1893. Moran, who lived from 1837 to 1926, had joined the Hayden Expedition in 1871, along with photographer William Henry Jackson. The purpose of the expedition was to determine the source of the Missouri and Yellowstone Rivers. Jackson and Moran were retained to document what the expedition encountered. The photographs taken by Jackson, along with some of Moran's paintings, prompted Congress to create Yellowstone National Park in 1872—the nation's first national park. Moran continued to create stunning works of art based on his trip for many years afterward, twenty-six in all, and these paintings include all the major scenic areas such as Lower Falls of the Yellowstone, Old Faithful, and Mammoth Hot Springs. Moran continued traveling throughout the West, capturing the vistas in a grand artistic style referred to as The Hudson River School of painting. I had seen images of some of these paintings since I was a child, though I had forgotten about them over time. Today I had already been to three of the settings he rendered so magnificently.

Glen Creek drops over 1,500 feet through the canyon and includes Rustic Falls near the top of the pass. The road, curving along the edge of the cliff, is supported by concrete arches, and the kiosk showed pictures from the late 1800s and early 1900s when the road was supported by a log trestle. We exited the car with our cameras just in time to capture the tanker truck going downhill and around the bend of the elevated roadway. We were in the shadow of clouds and rock walls, yet the sun had broken through to the valley beyond, so the view through the notch was quite impressive. The tanker provided the needed element of scale, and it was moving so fast we could only get one shot. It was worth the hair-raising stop.

Double tanker truck making the downhill curve at Golden Gate. **Yellowstone National Park Day 5**

Old Faithful was still a little over fifty miles away, and in this terrain, it was tough to judge how long that would take, but we knew we would probably be running short on daylight so we pressed on. Rain showers returned, as did the low clouds, but the view from the road as it wound through vast valleys of scrub grass and pine groves, along with more rock-strewn gorges and distant mountains, was nothing short of wonderful.

Pine trees in a valley, with bare stony mountains on both sides, and a welcome break in the rainy weather.

At one point the rain suddenly stopped, and the sun came out. I looked behind us to see a full rainbow and announced my sighting to Todd, who immediately swerved off to the opposite side of the road and into the entrance of some sort of muddy access road. We jumped out of the car to view the unexpected scene just as a van originating from the other direction did the same. A large, excited woman got out and breathlessly exclaimed, "We have been following this for the past ten minutes! Isn't it great?" We answered in the affirmative while focusing on getting a few photos. The odd thing about this rainbow was how low it appeared, and the short span from end to end. Maybe it had something to do with the altitude, relative low angle of the sun, or lateness of the year. It did not matter much, for it was another blessing from above, and added to the richness of our experience.

A rainbow over a high meadow, while clouds and rain obscure the mountains in the distance. West Loop Road. **Yellowstone National Park**

The road we were now following is considered the 'west loop,' which is not really a loop but more of a fat figure eight, and we were still around the top of the left (west) side of it. This side seemed to have even more geyser and vent activity than the east. Clouds of steam could be seen rising out of the woods in the distance, from mudflats nearby, and even along the small streams that the road ran parallel to. Some rated names, and a road to them, while others were just there to behold. Waterfalls were more prevalent as well. Some we could see as we zoomed along, but we did not stop at any. In fact, we did not stop at all until we encountered brake lights.

Bison in the middle of the road. They had the right-of-way and are much bigger than most cars.

    I was gazing out the passenger window when I felt us slowing down, and Todd said, "Uh oh, we have bison in the road."
    Sure enough, two huge brown furry beasts were ambling down the middle of the road. Cars were pulling off to get a better view, while the rest of the traffic attempted to get around both cars and beasts. The two cars ahead of us threaded their way through the chaos, and we followed. Todd rolled down his window for a better look as we crept along. We were looking straight out at the bottom of their bellies—they were that big. I yelled, "MOOOOOO!!" as we passed.

Todd started laughing, and said, "I don't know what that meant, but he did not like it!" while keeping an eye on the rearview mirror.

"Why? What happened?" I asked.

"He turned around and stopped the car behind us!"

"Good thing they are kind of slow, otherwise you would have had a buffalo head inside your window," I declared as we resumed speed, only to slow down again a couple of miles further along as carloads of Japanese tourists suddenly pulled to the side and jumped out to look at mule deer grazing in a small meadow.

The sky had become a steel-gray overcast when we arrived at Old Faithful around 5:30 PM, and the sun would set in about an hour. The whole complex was designed to handle large volumes of vehicles and people. There was even an overpass to funnel traffic in and out of the vicinity of the geyser. Due to the fact tourist season was virtually over, we followed the access roads and traversed vast empty parking lots to within two parking rows from the visitor center and the rear of the historic Old Faithful Inn.

The wind and rain arrived with a blast as we got out of the car and headed for the famous geyser. In the distance, we could see a steady plume of steam gently rising about fifty feet into the air before being blown away and dissipating.

Old Faithful, at rest.

"Is that it?" Todd asked, somewhat incredulous.

"Yup, that is it! But I think it is asleep right now."

"Good, I was going to ask for my money back! I wonder when it goes off again?"

I spotted a plastic sandwich-board style sign along the boardwalk surrounding the plaza and announced my findings. "We missed it by about ten minutes! Next eruption is in about eighty minutes, or around 6:40 PM."

"Okay. We came this far, and I really want to see this!"

"I agree, but I am not standing out here getting soaked and freezing for another hour. Let's go inside somewhere and wait. Besides, I really have to pee! Let's try the visitor center."

We walked over to the huge modern concrete-rustic style building, with really big windows, only to encounter a small hand-lettered sign taped to the door, "Closed."

"Well, that's just great! I have got to go! They don't even have the courtesy to say how long they are closed. Is it for an hour, or for the rest of the season?"

"So what do you suggest, brother? Going back to the car?" Todd asked while cupping his hands against the glass and peering into the darkened expanse.

"I think we ought to go over to that big old log inn and have a look around. Besides, I bet there is a restroom in there."

"How are we going to do that? We don't have a room or reservations."

"We walk in like we belong there!" I exclaimed. "Put some of that old alcoholic behavior to good use!"

Todd chuckled, and said, "Yeah, I can do that!"

Rear of The Old Faithful Inn, built of logs in 1903-1904.

Lobby of Old Faithful Inn, featuring the huge stone chimney with an iron clock, and log balconies on each floor.

The parking lot was at the rear of The Old Faithful Inn, and other than appearing to be quite big, gave little clue as to what it looked like inside. The more formal entrance was at the front, facing the meadow where the geysers vented and steamed. Built in 1903-1904, it is considered to be the largest log structure in the world. The lobby rises over four stories to the sharply pitched roof and is surrounded by log railing balconies on all the floors. Dominating the huge space is a freestanding stone chimney that rises to the roof, upon which is affixed an equally large hammered copper and wrought iron pendulum clock. The whole effect was quite stunning. Even the bathroom, with subway tile walls, mosaic tile floors, and varnished wood stalls, did not fail to impress with its aura of class. Equally important was the fact we were indoors and out of the wind and rain.

Acting like guests, instead of transients, we took advantage of the opportunity to sink into the large leather Mission Style sofas for a well needed moment of rest. Another, though much smaller, hand-hammered iron clock on a stone wall by the gift shop had its hands set to the time of the next anticipated eruption of the faithful geyser, 6:40 PM. The lobby hummed with the sounds of people arriving, going to the dining room, or merely traipsing around with necks craned up in wonder of this iconic creation.

Old Faithful Inn, front entrance portico, with namesake geyser in the distance.

Old Faithful performing.

People began to slowly migrate outside a little after 6:15 and assemble on the boardwalk while eyeing the steaming vent expectantly. A bit earlier than predicted, a few big puffs of vapor issued forth, then it rumbled and hissed as a column of hot water and steam rose about forty or fifty feet in the air. This lasted about three or four minutes before it died back down to an ordinary steaming vent. Less than overwhelming, but we were glad we waited to see it. Everyone hurried away as more dark clouds rolled over the hill to the west, and the cold driving rain returned. It was time to head back to Cody, Wyoming, and the comfort of our RV at The Ponderosa.

The drive would not be that simple though, for first we had to drive down to the West Thumb of Yellowstone Lake, which was twenty-seven miles, and take another road across the bottom of the imaginary figure eight. At that point, Cody was still another one hundred miles, and this would be driven in the rapidly darkening evening, and in blowing rain. Our best guess was that it would take about three-and-a-half to four hours, if we were lucky, which would put us in Cody somewhere between 10:30 to 11:30 PM. Todd was up to the task of Speed Racer, which is exactly how it went.

We made the turn at West Thumb and followed the west shore of the angry wind-whipped lake toward Lake Village and Fishing Bridge, by which time the dark of night had fully enveloped us. As my mother would sometimes say, it was "darker than the inside of a cow."

Todd managed to get around a few slow-moving cars and RVs, as well as other vehicles who were guilty of attempting the speed limit of 45 miles per hour. At some point a black VW Jetta passed us!

"Holy crap! What does this guy think he is doing?" Todd exclaimed while he watched the car's headlights approach in the side mirror, and then blow by us. Then he declared, "I'm sticking to him!", and floored the accelerator.

"I hope he is going the same direction as we are, because it is too dark to see anything!"

"As long as I can see his taillights, I can follow him!" Todd said with conviction.

The Jetta did turn toward Fishing Bridge, which meant he was heading toward Cody. The road at that point went nowhere else. The darkness and rain actually were helpful because all we could see was what was illuminated by the headlights, and not the steep drop-offs along the canyons and cliffs that we knew were out there in the blackness. A line of taillights and brake lights indicated a jam ahead. It was one of the long road construction areas, and we came back up behind the black mystery VW. The driver could take it no more and suddenly whipped to the left and began to pass the whole line of vehicles.

"Shit! He's going for it!" Todd followed suit. We passed at least a dozen cars, campers, and pickup trucks maneuvering along the mud, gravel, and potholed section of road. At the next section of construction, the Jetta did not even slow down. It just eased to the left and zoomed around everything crawling along. The zone was wide enough to slip between the slow traffic and a couple of oncoming vehicles, which surely must have caused them a moment of panic, especially since another pair of headlights belonging to our rental Hyundai was right behind him.

It was obvious that whoever was driving the black Jetta, they were intimately familiar with this road for they knew when to punch it to over 60 mph and when to back down or hit the brakes. Todd did not have that advantage, so most of the time the lead vehicle would get a quarter of a mile or more ahead. Periodically we would glimpse flickering taillights going through trees up or down in the distant black. A flash of brake lights indicated a curve ahead. When we were close enough to see the car and the sweep of its headlight beam, the curve would be fairly obvious, but when it was far ahead, the location of the curves and how sharp they were, was entirely unknown to us. The sign for the 8,530-foot summit at Sylvan Pass materialized like a specter, then flashed by. The Jetta kept racing ahead, and now the road was predominantly downward, but just as curvy. A couple of times we thought we had lost him. Then we would get a glimpse of his taillights only to find it was another vehicle, so Todd would pass them. He was driving on full instinct at times, which was rather nerve-racking for me. Close to the park entrance gates we caught back up to our leader, who did slow a bit to pass the guard station but not by much. Out of the park, the road slowly widened a bit and became relatively level, especially after we crossed a bridge over the North Fork of the Shoshone River. By this time the speeding Jetta had gotten almost a mile ahead, yet we would still catch fleeting glimpses of him in the distance as we crossed over the crests of low hills in the narrow valley. The last sighting was way in the distance as the road skirted the edge of Buffalo Bill Reservoir. The lights disappeared around a corner and he was gone. We came to the same corner, which curved through the long tunnel by the Buffalo Bill Dam, and then ran fairly straight down toward the lights of Cody. The Jetta was nowhere to be seen.

The road into Cody was dry. It looked like the rain had never made it over the last ridge of the mountains, and neither had the wind. Todd and I were starving, but we thought it best to fuel up the car first. It was a bit past 9:00 PM. By following the Jetta we had shaved over an hour and a half off the projected arrival time to Cody, which felt like a true miracle. There would have been no way to make that drive like that without the aid of our guide, and we were fully aware of that fact. Downtown Cody had closed for the evening. Only a high-class steakhouse and a Wendy's were still open. We opted for cheap fast food.

Stiffly exiting the car, after a tense and exhausting two-and-a-half-hour drive from the park in total darkness, the harsh fluorescent glare of the fast food joint was disorienting. Eating our burgers while staring about glassy-eyed, we spoke little, though when we did, it was in half-finished sentences expressing amazement regarding what we had seen this day and the fortuitous race in the dark out of the park. We were well aware of how lucky we had been, for if a bison, Big Foot, or some other large creature had wandered out on the road, we would not be enjoying the minimal conversation we were having, and would be in a much different resting place. When we returned to the RV, we both retired immediately, and the lights were out before ten.

Chapter 9
Free Range

Friday, October 5- Day 6

For some unknown reason, I woke up a little after 4:00 AM. After the full and exhausting day, we had yesterday, I fully anticipated sleeping in until at least five or six. But it was obvious I was really awake, so I decided I may as well get up and head for the shower house. To my surprise, it was snowing lightly, and just starting to stick to the cars and picnic tables but melted when it hit the ground. The air was dead calm, so the walk to the shower was pleasant, and actually serene in the gently falling snow. Although it was 32°, it did not feel bad at all. When I returned, I made coffee, then went outside to the protection of the log shelter over our picnic table. During the customary early morning phone call to Tammy, I provided her with a brief description of our day yesterday in Yellowstone, leaving out the death-defying road experiences, and informed her it was snowing as we spoke. She said it was supposed to be near 80° again back in Ohio, and since it had been so nice overnight, our four cats had stayed out all night.

Early mornings alone are peaceful, especially this one. The wonder and miracle of yesterday hung on strong. Gently falling snow was a perfect exclamation point to it all. I was able to share a bit of this sensation with my best friend and partner over the phone. Wanting to immerse myself in the experience a while longer, I fixed another cup of coffee and a bowl of cereal and enjoyed both in quiet contemplation.

View from our campsite at the Ponderosa RV Park in Cody, Wyoming, with fresh snow in the mountains to the west toward Yellowstone National Park, where we had just visited the day before .Day 6

While Todd got the RV ready to roll, I went down to Walmart for another couple more of jugs of water, then headed to Yellowstone Regional Airport to drop off the rental car. At first, no one was there, and I was planning on just leaving the car and hoped they would figure it out, but finally, the rental franchise owner walked in and we settled up proper like. Todd was sitting outside in the RV when this transaction was concluded.

Originally our plan was to go back into Yellowstone and then head south to Grand Teton National Park and go pick up Interstate 80 somewhere over in Idaho and continue west. However, having driven some of those roads yesterday, we knew that Yellowstone was no place for a large RV. Also, as we were checking out of The Ponderosa, Larry had said some of the roads in Yellowstone were now closed due to snow! God had smiled upon us again! In the morning light we could see a light coating of snow on the mountains just west of Cody, and the gap.

So, we had to come up with Plan B. Now we would head south-southeast and try to get around the snow zone, and then zig-zag over to I-80 at Rock Springs, near the southwestern Wyoming border. We were currently in the northwest part of the state. Actually, there were no alternatives in this state of few roads and lots of mountain ranges. The state map we had was a relief map, showing the mountains and deserts, but even that was a bit misleading. We really needed to be heading west, but our choices were dictated by what we were driving, the minimal route options available, and most importantly, the weather.

That meant we had to head south. No point dithering about it—time to hit the road.

Light dusting of snow on the hills and distant mountains, while heading southeast of Cody on Route 120

Route 120 heading southeast out of Cody, toward mountains in the distance. Our Wyoming Highway map with relief features did not really indicate what was in store for us for the next couple of hundred miles—more mountains and crossing the Continental Divide.

Route 120 started just west of the Yellowstone Regional Airport and ran south-southeast toward a town called Thermopolis. The relief map made it look like the road followed several broad valleys and over some low hills. As we started out, the primary notable feature was the snow tinged mountain range to the west toward Yellowstone. They slowly got farther away and were obscured by the nearby hills. To the east, snow-covered buttes came into view. It had been partly sunny, but we could see low hanging clouds on the hills to the south. As we got closer, the clouds and the hills took on a more ominous look. The hills became mountains, and the straight road was no longer that. It now was sweeping up and down within ever deepening valleys and skirting large round mountains. We encountered an overhead electronic road-condition sign declaring fog ahead, as well as high wind. Thirty seconds later the road rounded a curve on the side of a massive round hill and ascended into the thick clouds. Spaced at intervals along the road were windsocks, identical to those at airports, so motorists could gauge the direction and strength of the wind. A couple of electronic signs stated the now obvious wind and fog, and they had gates to close the road. Fortunately, the gates were open.

Thermopolis was a nice size town down in a valley out of the clouds. A state park was nearby with a hot spring, hence the name of the town. Substantial masonry buildings two and three stories tall in the two-block downtown indicated this was once a place of some import, but whatever that was had faded away, and now most of the storefronts were vacant.

We changed routes here and picked up RT-789 and US-20 which headed south and crossed the Big Horn River, then headed upstream along the attractive narrow river.

Our trusty state map gave little clue what we would see from this road. A few miles south of town a two-lane asphalt began a descent into the Wind River Canyon of the Big Horn River through the Owl Creek Mountains. The stony river was no more than one hundred feet wide, fringed by a thin line of box elder trees. On the west bank were the tracks of the BNSF Railway, and on the other side was the road. That was all there was room for, except occasional sidetracks down to the river for fishermen and campers. Sheer rock walls rose higher and higher the further we wound down into the canyon. Eventually they were towering over a thousand feet on either side. The road rates a "Scenic By-Way" designation on the state map, which was a total understatement, for it was truly stunning. At one point the canyon was so narrow both the road and the railroad went through several tunnels on their respective sides. Suddenly exiting the gorge, we were confronted with a flat expanse of land and Boysen Reservoir, created by a dam at the neck of the canyon. RT-789 followed the shore of the lake for miles. The other side of the road was dry scrub grass and sagebrush, and not much else. Water, land, but no trees. A highly unusual tableau for a couple of Midwest guys to wrap their heads around. When the road came to the town of Riverton, it again crossed the Big Horn River, and the land became sharply rolling and hilly covered by short scrub. How dramatically the landscape changed from one mile to the next never ceased to amaze us.

Wyoming Route 789 / US-20 crossing the Big Horn River just south of Thermopolis, and about to enter Wind River Canyon. A truly spectacular drive. **Day 6**

Road closure gate, before the road enters the Wind River Canyon. Although the road descended sharply, the Big Horn River is flowing in the opposite direction, creating a strange optical illusion. **Day 6**

Snowy mountains above the Wind River Canyon, as the road winds up-stream, even though it is headed down, along the barely visible Big Horn River, on the right. **Day 6**

Wind River Canyon of the Big Horn River. Three tunnels ahead for the road, and for the Burlington Northern Santa Fe Railroad on the opposite side of the river, as the gorge narrows. A dam at the end of the canyon creates Boysen Reservoir, covering a vast area of flat plateau just beyond the tunnels. **Day 6**

A small village named Hudson had the appearance of a perfectly preserved frontier town. A small sign stated, "Leaving the Wind River Indian Reservation." We did not know we had even been on an Indian reservation. A low stucco building still sported a 1920s vintage painted advertisement on its side touting, "Pennzoil – manufactured over millions of years in the mountains of Pennsylvania," and included a fine rendering of a brontosaurus to establish the point. The few other vacant buildings gave evidence of being a bank, general store, and a hotel. A vacant two-story building had "Rooms" painted on the front above the upper windows. The last paying customer decamped decades ago. Another predominant feature of this town was the use of round river rocks. They filled many of the yards, in the place of grass, lined the streets between the pavement and sidewalks, and were stacked into artistic piles here and there. Rocks were placed everywhere. The resulting effect was that Hudson was perfect to be the set for a weird David Lynch movie, which in this case was rather intriguing. As with other towns we encountered, there was no transition—it was the town, then a continuation of the desolate large brown hills. The dirt side streets, some trimmed with round river rocks, made the transition even more abrupt.

Todd had been playing with the satellite mapping device, now connected to his phone, while he was driving, and found an old road that bypassed the next town where we were supposed to change routes.

"This looks quicker!" he declared as he swerved left off the state route and on to a road that would hardly rate as a township road in Ohio. It was barely two lanes, so the big RV took up most of the pocked and crumbling pavement. This road was probably the original paved road before the more modern graded state route, which we had abruptly left, was constructed. We did get an 'up close and personal' view of a couple of ranches, but it was hard to discern what their primary source of income was, for they were devoid of both crops and livestock, yet they had nice barns and silos for both. The road eventually ended at a U.S. highway, a short distance from the state route we wanted to be on. It had proved to be a fine shortcut and by-passed the town of Lander. Whether that was a good thing, we shall never know.

Route 28 was another of the great Wyoming highways. We concluded that since there are so few roads in the state, they spare no expense in making them smooth, wide, and well graded. A sign at the intersection stated it was heading for a town called Farson. We had encountered several other signs previously indicating the route to Farson, so we were getting the impression this must be an important place.

As it turned out, Farson was still over 68 miles away and the route was quickly taking us back up into the clouds. For the second time today, there were electronic signs again warning of fog and wind and accompanied by gates. The fog turned to a heavy mist, which turned to snow. The wind picked up as well, before we passed the first windsock. Out of the cloud and snow appeared a road sign pointing to a town called South Pass City and then another one, pointing in the same direction, toward a town called Atlantic City, as well as a notation that they were both "historic." In this weather, we were not stopping for anything, and we were starting to wonder whether we would actually make it to the alluring Farson, Wyoming alive, or be forced to turn around by one of those sinister gates. A few miles further appeared a sign stating, "South Pass – elevation 7,980 feet."

I read this information to Todd as the sign swept by, and declared, "Damn! We are almost as high as some of the passes yesterday in Yellowstone!"

"You're kidding! I cannot see a doggone thing!"

Looks are deceiving. We had just crossed over the Rocky Mountains and the Continental Divide at South Pass, elevation 7,980 feet. The pass was in the clouds, accompanied by wind, fog, and snow.

The road began a steep curvy descent, and on either side was brown grass. For such a high pass we expected rocks, so this was unlike any other mountain we had previously encountered. The snow suddenly stopped, and then we drove out of the bottom of the clouds. It became partly sunny, with blue sky poking through. Just as quickly there appeared a small and very new rest area. It also served as an improved turnaround for travelers heading up the mountain, in the event they encountered the gates closed.

Todd had been driving since we left Cody, and he needed a break, and for the first time on this expedition he suggested I take over driving. I took a picture of the nearby clouds hugging the top of the mountain and read an information kiosk about the significance of the South Pass of the Wind River Range on the old Oregon Trail during the mid-1800s. There also was info about the two towns whose signs we had recently seen, but I had neither the time nor the stamina against the cold wind to read it all. It made me want to come back another time and see some of this stuff when I had more time and was in a vehicle that was not so big. The fact pioneers found this area to be the easiest route to travel across indicated how rugged the alternative routes were. I tried to imagine the supreme effort required to get a covered wagon through places like this. Driving it on a nice road was challenge enough. And until I read the historical marker, I had no idea we had just crossed the Continental Divide and the Rocky Mountains! Although we had been in the clouds, and could only see some grass, it had been apparent that we were driving through and over some big stuff. It made sense now, the pioneers on the Oregon Trail crossed the Rockies where it was not rocky, and relatively easy compared to any of their other options, but it was definitely high.

Route 28 heading for Farson, Wyoming, after descending from South Pass. A remarkable change from the wind and snow encountered less than an hour previously when crossing the pass. The flat-topped butte and distant mountains are all over 8,000 feet in height. Along the lonely scenic road, the ever-present short brown wiry scrub grass.

Same butte as the previous photo only from many more miles down the road, yet the feel of the scenery and the clouds create an ever-changing panorama. Wyoming Route 28 between South Pass and greater metropolitan Farson.

The road transitioned to an expanse of very flat land toward Farson. The first indication we were re-entering civilization was a small single-story school to the side of the road. Being Friday, there was a high school football game going on, except it was during regular school hours. The school was so small and basic there were no lights for a night game, and only two dozen people filled one low bleacher. Where they came from was impossible to guess, for we had not seen any houses, or roads for that matter, in almost an hour. The last sign for a town was before we crossed over South Pass, yet here was a high school football game being played. Small wonder that there were only about six kids in uniform on each team.

The sign welcoming us to greater metropolitan Farson, Wyoming was just past the school. To call Farson a town was a true stretch of the term. It was a cluster of raggedy mobile homes set every which way amid some scraggly small trees, plus a couple of big windowless metal industrial looking buildings of undefined purpose. A large plain cinder-block building housed a gas station and a rudimentary market, set amidst a big patch of gravel at the only intersection, which was demarcated by a very large stop sign at the crossroad. The view in any direction was at least five to ten miles of unobstructed scrub and sagebrush. Straight ahead, Route 28 downsized from a very nice road to a small strip of pavement heading straight toward the horizon. The crossroad was US-191, which we actually had planned to take south to Rock Springs and Interstate 80. Being the first gas station, we had encountered in a couple of hours, we figured we better stop for fuel. Judging by the looks of the area, and by the emptiness of the land we just driven through, this might be our only chance for a long while. Besides, we had finally reached the grand metropolis of Farson! We had to stop, just to say we had been there.

The RV crunched through the gravel to the fuel pumps. Todd wondered aloud, "Wonder what would happen if we just kept going straight? It's going more in the direction we want than this other road, isn't it?"

"From here, it certainly looks like it does, but who knows? Let's ask inside," I said with a shrug.

The gas station/store had the usual crap jammed on to shelves around the front counter, which was apparently manned by the owner, a husky young man of about thirty. He had the air of propriety about him, despite sporting a scruffy short beard, sweatshirt, ball cap, and a wad of tobacco stuck behind his lower lip. He was talking with the authority of a 'person in-the-know' to a couple of women who had stopped by for snacks and gossip. The rest of the store was a long low room with metal shelves, which were mostly empty, save for a package of toilet paper here, a couple of cans of soup there, and some dish soap in another aisle on another primarily empty shelf. I found a coffee pot on a hotplate, partly full of steaming dark brown fluid of unknown vintage and filled my travel mug while listening to the conversation up at the counter. Waylon Jennings and Willie Nelson blared from an unseen radio. "This is all too stereotypical and classic," I thought to myself, but not in a negative or judgmental way, for I had gained a true appreciation of both these musicians when I bartended in a shit-kicker bar just up the street from my apartment in my hometown, decades ago. Had I not known who was singing, I would not have appreciated this "life imitating art" moment quite so much and would have been standing in judgement of these people and this place. I waited my turn to get a carton of cheap Winston cigarettes and pay for my cup of hot driving fuel. There was time to scope out the slim selection of typical convenient store junk, and I was tempted to grab the ball cap with the moniker, "Where the HELL is Farson, Wyoming?" stitched across the front. This lonely hat, the only one on display, was in hot pink. I had already purchased a fine cap back at The Badlands, so I resisted. The gossip ended, the ladies left, and it was my turn at the counter.

"So, what is up with Route 28 if you keep going straight that way?" I asked while motioning west across the intersection.

"What do you mean?"

"Well, we just came from the other direction and it is a rather nice road, but on the other side here, it obviously changes into something entirely different. So, like, how far does it go?"

"You definitely do not want to drive it at night!" the man declared in all seriousness.

"Well, how about right now?" I asked, rather taken aback, and perplexed by his curious response.

"What are you driving?"

"That big land yacht at the fuel pump!" I replied, with a wave toward the window.

He leaned over to scrutinize the vehicle and grimaced. Waylon and Willie continued to keep the beat in the background while he considered the facts. "If you leave right now you should be okay," he stated with assurance, then added, "but what you have to understand is, that is 'free range area' out there. There are no fences, and the cattle are starting to head to the road for winter. Everything else is out there too, especially antelope! So watch out for animals on the road."

"Okay, I appreciate the info," I said. Then to get some clarification, asked, "So how far does this road go?"

"Oh, about thirty miles or so to the next road. But all that area out there is 'free range,'" he said while handing me my change.

I reported my findings to Todd as I got back into the driver's seat and readjusted the mirrors.

"Well, all right!" Todd exclaimed. "That ought to be interesting to see, don't ya' think?"

"Sounds cool to me!" I said, "And we have thirty-some miles for you to figure out how we get out of this state, or at least get headed in a more westerly direction. You're the navigator! And try to give me some advance notice of any road changes, if you would be so kind!"

Soon after crossing the intersection, we crossed over cattle grates in the road. What appeared to have been a straight road quickly began winding along dry washes and low rises. About a mile into the unknown, a large billboard sized sign declared "FREE RANGE," along with a life-size silhouette of a cow. Thereafter, about every three miles a similar sign would appear, only with a different animal outline, like an antelope — which included the additional advisory of "crossing at 55 mph!" Other signs were for grouse, then elk, and then they repeated a cow. Apparently, this was sufficient warning. Drivers would have either hit one of those species or would now be exercising sufficient caution. We did not see any cattle but did see several antelope, and a grouse flew up from the side of the road and ceased living with a BANG! into the windshield.

The loud avian hari-kari briefly roused Todd from his nap with a, "What the hell was that?"

"That was a grouse! The operative phrase being, was!"

"Damn! How big was it?"

"About the size of a very large chicken!"

"You know, they had signs back there warning about that kind of shit," Todd advised while reclining back into his seat and pulling his cap over his eyes to resume his nap.

The road was devoid of any human habitation or presence. There were no houses, no power lines, no guard rails, and no signs other than the animal warnings. There was barely the trace of a faded centerline. Occasionally, however, there would be a historic marker along the side of the road. Most of them were denoting some massacre, but since I was rolling along at about 70 mph, it was not possible to discern who was killing whom. The land was arid, and only supported the same wiry brown tufts of short grass and clumps of sagebrush, so it was hard to fathom why anyone would be killing each other for this land, let alone even be out here for any reason other than to pass through it. Maybe it was the passing through by the early pioneers that resulted in the various massacres, since the other markers were regarding The Oregon Trail. We were heading for Oregon ourselves, so I took those as a good indication that we must be on the right track somehow.

Several times the road crested the edge of a plateau to provide a vista of the road heading off to the horizon dozens of miles in the distance. Periodically these types of vantage points also had the low faint outlines of mountains on the horizon, but most of the time the rolling land seemed to go on forever. It was a truly remarkable drive through arid total isolation.

Incongruously, in this expanse of sagebrush and scrub, we crossed a mean and deep appearing stream called The Green River. It was actually brown, and maybe a little over sixty feet wide. There were no trees to denote its passage across the barren landscape.

Thirty miles to the south, the original Transcontinental Railroad, which was the Central Pacific Railroad through these parts, crossed this river. The crossing resulted in the namesake town of Green River. On May 24, 1869, a one-armed Civil War major named John Wesley Powell began the last great quest of the American West. Maps of that era denoted a large expanse of the lands to the southwest as 'unexplored.' Major Powell intended to rectify that situation. The ultimate goal was to explore the fabled Colorado River through the Grand Canyon. The rough and desolate town of Green River, Wyoming was chosen as the jumping off point for this expedition. It was selected not for its proximity to the Colorado River, which it is not, but because shipping four wooden rowboats and supplies for ten men by rail from Chicago to the town of Green River, was faster and easier than overland in wagons to a point nearer the Colorado River. The

Green River joins the Colorado River a little over one hundred miles downriver of the town. Powell's journey of exploration began two weeks after the dedication of the completion of the Transcontinental Railroad, by the driving of The Golden Spike at Promontory Summit, Utah on May 10, 1869. The Native Americans knew the Green River well, and about the canyons and rapids it went through, and had advised the one-armed Major two years earlier to forget about the boat ride. He went anyway, and many of the places his party named remain on the map today. Had I known about its importance in the larger scheme of things, as the RV rolled over the small bridge, I would have paid more attention to this strange out-of-place river, which originates on the western side of the Continental Divide in the Wind River Range of the Rocky Mountains.

When we finally came to another road there was little or no warning. I had to wake Todd from his slumber to ask which way to go, which he did after looking at his phone-satellite navigation gizmo, and then he would resume his comfortable posture. Other than the appearance of some large oil well pump-jacks, the changes in route from RT-28 to RT-372, and then US-189, offered more of the same for another hour or so, except the outlines of the mountains slowly got larger and closer. The U.S. route was a slightly better road, in that it had a painted line down the center and a bit more of a berm on each side.

Todd's new objective, according to his phone, was a town named Kemmerer. This would be where we would get on the original cross-country highway of US-30, which in some parts of the country, like in Ohio, is still referred to as The Lincoln Highway. We had crossed the US-30 / Lincoln Highway on Day Two back at our fuel stop at Missouri City, Iowa. Later inspection of the Rand McNally Road Atlas, and much to my personal disappointment, showed that US-30 left the route of the Lincoln Highway just west of Green River, which then angled southwest toward its ultimate destination of the Golden Gate Bridge in San Francisco, California. None of this would mean much except to a map and geography nerd like myself. The Lincoln Highway was conceived in 1913 as one route from coast to coast, crossing thirteen states and 3,389 miles in length, to promote highway travel. In fact, it was not a new road, but a route stitched together of existing roads connecting town to town. Road markers with a large "L" on a red, white, and blue rectangle denoted the route. Guidebooks were created to induce the county's citizenry to get in their automobiles and hit the road, even though most Americans did not own a car at the time. At the turn of the century, there were only 150 miles of paved road, outside of cities, in the whole country. By 1913, not much had improved. Carl G. Fischer, the founder of the Indianapolis Motor Speedway, and Henry B. Joy, president of the Packard Motor Car Company saw this coast to coast highway as a fitting memorial to President Abraham Lincoln, hence the name Lincoln Highway. In 1919, a young Lieutenant Colonel named Dwight D. Eisenhower joined an Army convoy on a trek across the United States, from Washington D.C. to San Francisco. The purpose was to test the mobility of the military during wartime conditions, and they followed the Lincoln Highway all the way. What they found was that the highway was in name only. Roads were rarely paved, except in some towns, in the early twentieth century. The trucks got stuck in mud and sand the whole way, and the trip took sixty-two days. This journey left a lasting impression on the young officer, as did encountering German high-speed Autobahn roadways during World War II. As President, Dwight Eisenhower signed a bill in 1953 to create the Interstate Highway System. It took forty years to complete all the envisioned routes, not including by-passes and short inner-city connectors required by increasing traffic volumes. The Lincoln Highway, and more than 80 other similarly named routes, which were maintained and promoted independently, lasted until the early 1920s when the Federal Government embarked on a road numbering system. US-30 generally follows the westward path of the original Lincoln Highway all the way into Wyoming at Green River. From there other numbered routes followed the route to California, while US-30 veers off toward Portland, Oregon by following parts of the old Oregon Trail used by the pioneers. Today, in Wyoming, Interstate 80 still proudly wears the banner of the Lincoln Highway and was built over much of the original route. I knew our rendezvous with US-30 had some historical connotation but was wrong about which one. As with so many other points of interest on this journey, we would miss the Lincoln Highway by about forty miles but would find ourselves on the old pioneer track of the Oregon Trail instead, so it was all good.

    Kemmerer was a small prosperous looking town, evidenced by the well-kept houses on small lots, packed into the tight valley of an attractive looking stream, which was lined with trees and real looking greenish grass. The town's main feature was a small railyard for the Union Pacific Railroad. Also, we were suddenly back in the realm of large mountains.

US-30, along with the railroad, wound through a gap at Fossil Butte and descended more than 2,000 feet in nineteen miles from Kemmerer to Cokeville. Todd was now awake to take in the stunning scene, which included 6% grades, twisting canyons, and towering mountains. Along this route we passed several Oregon Trail historical markers, and at one point we saw the actual ruts that the wheels of hundreds of covered wagons had dug into the side of a hill over 150 years ago. Decades earlier I had read in a *National Geographic* magazine that this evidence still existed in places of the arid west. Actually seeing them was a true thrill. The highway abruptly exited the mountains and entered a picturesque valley that swung from a northerly direction to westerly as it entered the state of Idaho.

Initially, there did not seem to be much difference between Idaho and Wyoming, though the former was a bit more populous. Lots of rock and grass-covered mountains in every direction, and the few houses were accompanied by the ever-present big stacks of large hay bales. However, the further we got into Idaho the towns and villages became more numerous, and had things like sidewalks, fenced yards, and traffic lights. In one town I was driving a bit too fast to even bother trying to slow down as the light turned from yellow to red.

I looked over at Todd, and declared, "Well, that one was a little orange! I shall stop twice at the next traffic light I come to!"

He chuckled, and said, "I was wondering if you saw that because you were rolling along pretty good!"

"These towns creep up on you pretty fast especially after spending most of the day out in the middle of nowhere doing seventy miles an hour! I definitely need to dial it down a notch now that we seem to have returned to civilization," I said as I eased the RV up to a more respectable 65 mph upon leaving the pocket of civilization.

At Lava Hot Springs, Idaho we stopped for a much-needed break and fueled the RV. Now down to a well-synchronized routine, Todd fueled while I cleaned glass. I had time to take a couple of pictures, for this was the first time since we left Cody in the morning that there was real green grass and healthy-looking pine trees. It was getting late back in Ohio, due to being late afternoon here, so I gave Tammy a quick call to report our progress. We switched drivers when we completed the service stop and were soon rolling again.

Western-style long double trailer tanker truck passing by Lava Hot Springs, Idaho. A strange sight for a couple of Midwesterners.

Mountainous southeastern Idaho at Lava Hot Springs, on US-30, following the old Oregon Trail used by the pioneers.

Buff colored, grass-covered mountains in southeast Idaho, viewed from Interstate 15. The solitude of the lonely two-lane roads was missed, but the scenery was still grand. Heavy traffic, skid marks, and a construction zone welcomed us back to civilization and high-speed Interstate traveling.

A broad valley and mountains in southeastern Idaho, and the route of I-15 toward Pocatello. **Day 6**

US-30 joined I-15 at McCammon, Idaho and we headed north toward Pocatello. The road was in a nice wide valley with pine trees growing halfway up the rock crowned mountains. Although we could make time and miles on the Interstate, I regretted having to leave the two-lane roads. For one thing, they are more scenic, and one feels closer to the land. Another thing is less traffic. For most of the drive this day we only encountered a couple of vehicles in an hour if that. Now we were back in the close proximity of metal hurling along at more than a mile a minute, piloted by persons of questionable skill and concentration.

I-86 headed west from Pocatello, and then turned into I-84 as we drilled across the state of Idaho in fading light. Mountains could be seen to the south of us, and periodically we could catch a glimpse of the Snake River on our right, but mostly we saw large hay fields irrigated by huge crawling sprinklers. Pocatello, a rather old industrial looking place, was visible from the Interstate, but the rest of the cities in this state were completely bypassed by the big road. There were not even any gas stations at the exit ramps, just a sign for whatever burg lay hidden beyond the hayfields or tree lines. There was a gentle roll to the land, but as the sun set and darkness took over, we had the feeling we were not missing much. This was definitely not the scenic part of this state. Rows of mysterious blinking red lights provided a diversion for a while. We never did figure out what those were all about and concluded they probably had something to do with space aliens.

Exhaustion gnawed at my consciousness as I stared ahead at the small patch of pavement, illuminated by our headlights, sweeping beneath us. I suggested to Todd that we ought to find an RV park and call it a day. At one point he agreed, so we exited and followed signs toward a park. We did find a small industrial town, that was now fast asleep, but no further evidence of a campground or park. As a matter of fact, there were no eating establishments of any kind either, which was a disappointing development, for we had not eaten since breakfast more than twelve hours earlier.

When we were driving the Interstate Highway earlier in the trip, Todd and I would usually fix ourselves something to eat when we switched drivers. That is an advantage of being in an RV. The vehicle does not have to stop in order for someone to eat or pee, unless that someone happens to be the driver. On this day there was too much to look at, and watch out for, so the only stops we had made were to switch drivers or get fuel. The rest of the time it was all forward progress, even if we were not necessarily heading in the optimal direction, and the scenery was too compelling to waste time getting something to eat because we might miss something.

Todd seemed to be energized by the force of determination following our failure to find a place of rest or sustenance. Much earlier in the day, before we left Cody, I had mentioned it would actually be possible for us to spend some time at the Pacific Ocean before we had to deliver the RV to Amy on Monday. I also had said, that according to the Rand McNally, there were a lot of state parks along this stretch of Interstate through Idaho and into Oregon.

At the time, Todd seemed shocked that the ocean was a possibility. Now he was set on making sure that it was a certainty, and in order for that to happen, he now wanted to get out of this state before we stopped, or at least be very close to the Oregon border. There were still over two hundred miles to go and stopping at any state park along the way apparently vanished.

Fatigue started to win over again, and we decided to search the billboards for a campground as we approached the prosaically named town of Mountain Home. It had an appealing name, and we both recalled there was some sort of state park nearby, but we did not want to get blinded by turning on a light in order to look at the map and find out. The area became appropriately hilly, with trees down to the edge of the highway, but no billboards offered the service we desired, which was a place to park this beast and get some much-needed rest.

"Fuck 'em!" Todd declared, "I'm going to drive all night to get out of this state!"

After a while, signs of civilization became more prevalent, in the form of lights in the distance, and then a glow in the sky in the direction we were heading. This was the suburban sprawl of Boise, Idaho. Then we actually could see downtown Boise, beyond the tangle of freeways joining and departing I-84, which at one point was ten lanes wide. The sight of that made us glad we were passing through late at night. Rush hour traffic must be a bitch in this city. Why else did they need such huge freeways? More suburban cities formed an endless chain as we proceeded west. Metro area Boise was truly expansive and was even more impressive since this was the biggest urban area we had encountered since the first day of the trip back in the Midwest. We remarked on the size of this place, and the fact my daughter and grandkids lived out there somewhere in the urban sprawl. Todd suggested we drop-in and see them. I countered that we probably would get the RV stuck in the suburbs, or in a cul-de-sac, and we would be lost forever.

Finally, Todd remarked, "There has got to be a truck stop out here somewhere! It's about time to stop. I can probably make it to the Oregon line, but not much further."

"To tell you the truth, I have not seen any signs for truck stops, just advertising for food and great deals on houses," I replied, thankful he was finally willing to throw in the towel.

A bit later Todd got off at an isolated exit. I had not seen any sign, and he had not mentioned one, so maybe it was an act of desperation. Across the bridge over the Interstate was the glow of a Sinclair gas station, and with the exception of the light from our headlights, was the only light piercing the blackness. A short distance ahead the road came to a dead-end, so the fuel station was the only place to go. As it turned out, the Sinclair fuel station was also The Stinker Truck Stop at Exit #13 at Black Canyon. There was a small single-story 'no-tell motel,' with a restaurant, adjacent to the truck stop. Unfortunately, the restaurant was closed. We did the service routine and using an extra-long window squeegee made for trucks, I was finally able to clean off a bunch of spider webs that had collected over the rearview camera and had been driving Todd nuts all evening.

Truck parking was in a gravel lot behind the fuel and supplies building. Todd wheeled the RV to the back of the lot, then swung around to an isolated location by a row of trees. We extended one of the sliders so I could unfold the hide-a-bed. Todd nuked some hotdogs in the microwave, which we gratefully ate in silence before collapsing into our respective beds. Small wonder, it was around 11 PM and we had been driving since 9 AM, and covered a little over 760 miles, 450 of which had been on two-lane roads. We had been in clouds and snow twice, almost crossed two states, been in canyons, mountains, and had experienced total isolation in the west. It had been quite a day.

Chapter 10
The Pacific

Saturday, October 6- Day 7

Rising from my slumber a little before 6 AM meant I had really slept in, so I must have been tired. It was a cool, calm morning, and still dark as night, as I walked up to the truck stop building to take a shower. The fee was five dollars. I balked at this perceived bit of larceny at first, then becoming aware of my aching body, thought better of it, and gladly handed over a Lincoln for a shower key. Since I had my own towel and washcloth, I avoided the extra fee for those necessities and felt sorry for the poor over-the-road truckers forced to hand over ten bucks to get clean and refreshed. A shower and a shave has remarkable restorative powers, and after a long day and night like yesterday, I needed all the magic the process could provide.

The sky was starting to brighten, and a few stray drops of rain could be felt, when I went back outside to have a smoke and a cup of coffee and call Tammy. She was distraught when she answered. She had coughed up blood in the morning. I tried to comfort her by saying it was probably okay, since she was recovering from a two-week bout of bronchitis, and a little bit of blood was natural under those circumstances. She was hearing none of that because she was sure she was dying! I suggested she go over to Diley Ridge Hospital Emergency Room to be checked out. This did not sit well at all. I was supposed to be with her to go to an emergency room to find out she had cancer, and it was all my fault that I was not home to comfort her. Then she hung up. "Oh, great!" I thought to myself. "I will not hear the end of this, no matter what happens," and walked back in the RV.

Todd was primed to head across Oregon to the Pacific Ocean. I suggested maybe we ought to check the coolant level of the engine before we made this final push, and he agreed it would be prudent. It was a good thing we checked because we had to add over a gallon to the coolant reservoir. We were on the road by 7 AM, and Todd was back at the wheel.

Rain and fog descended shortly after we resumed our westward trek. What we could not see last night, but now could in the dim misty light, was that we were in a hilly area of tall pine trees. We crossed the Snake River and were now in Oregon. At this point the land briefly widened out along the river, but that soon changed to huge rolling hills and mountains covered with short buff-colored grass. I-84/US-30 angled northwest across the northeastern part of the state. The road climbed up and down mountains and through narrow passes. Railroad tracks followed the same route, sometimes along the road, and other times far below in a valley. It turned out that we were still basically following The Oregon Trail of pioneer days. Around Baker City, which looked rather small to call a city, the road was back into another broad valley and pine trees reappeared. Farming continued to be hay, but also some sort of short looking corn. More miles and miles of rolling buff-colored hills for the next two hours. These were western hills, not Ohio hills. They were huge, rising over a thousand feet, creating valleys a mile wide, which made the road and the trains appear positively small. The size and expanse of the West has to be experienced to be appreciated. There is nothing to compare it to.

Day 7 I-84 near the Idaho-Oregon border, in rain and fog. Green trees at last, but soon the landscape would change again.

One of the many Burlington Northern Santa Fe railroad trains seen along I-84 in eastern Oregon.

I-84 in the eastern portion of the Columbia River Gorge, which extends over 100 miles to Portland, Oregon. **Day 7**

The road dropped down into the Columbia River Gorge to follow the river west toward the still distant ocean. The rain had stopped, so we just enjoyed the view. Once again, everything was on a stupendously large scale. A river valley half a mile wide. Hills and cliffs on either side rising at least fifteen hundred feet above the river. Brown grass as far as the eye could see across the tops of the hills.

During this time Tammy called back to inform me she had taken herself to the emergency room. "See! I can take care of myself! I don't need you!" the angry voice admonished from two thousand miles away.

"I knew you could do it. You are a strong person."

"That's not the point! You should have been here with me! What if it *is* cancer?!"

"What have they told you?" I asked, trying to sound reasonable and reassuring at the same time.

"Nothing! I am waiting for an X-ray."

"Well, let me know what they say. I do care."

"Yeah, right!" replied my displeased wife. "If you cared, you would be here, and I would not have to go through this by myself!" and then hung up.

I put my phone away, shook my head in perplexed amazement, and looked out the window at the foreign landscape passing by.

"Troubles with the little lady?" Todd asked with exaggerated fake empathy. I had already told him about the previous conversation.

"Yes, and no," I replied. "Tammy has managed to drag herself to the hospital. No word on a diagnosis, but it is all my fault."

"Of course, it is!"

I thought about the vast difference between the calls Todd had versus the ones I had. Mostly he talked to his son Noah about taking his driver's license test, which he passed, and then about going to his football homecoming dance. The calls to Margy, from the front of the RV, were rather mundane. Calls at night from the back bedroom, I could not hear, but I highly doubted they were as angst-filled as mine.

"You all right over there?" Todd asked, breaking my depressing thoughts.

"Yeah, I'm good. I am here experiencing this," I replied as I waved across the view out the windshield, "and not home dealing with that, whatever *that* is."

Half an hour later Tammy called back, and much calmer, to say there was no cancer or anything else on the chest X-rays. Any blood she was coughing up was probably the result of the bronchitis and would go away in a few days. I thanked her for the update and told her I was glad that was all it was.

The landscape of light brown short grass covering the impressively large round hills on either side of the Columbia River continued, only now the gorge was getting deeper. The combined route of I-84 & US-30 ran on the south bank, along with tracks of the Union Pacific Railroad. The river, at least a quarter-mile wide, got even wider above several large dams. On the north bank is the Burlington Northern Santa Fe (BNSF) Railroad and a state highway. Train traffic on both sides was mainly heading upstream, pulled by at least four locomotives and one or two pusher engines on the rear to shove the long trains out of the gorge and over the mountains in eastern Oregon. The number of trains was quite impressive, and they appeared to be running about ten miles apart. Most of the trains were stack trains of shipping containers, but also there were a number of mixed manifest freight trains as well, with a lot of lumber racks in them which kept the train viewing more interesting.

The distance from where the highway entered the deep valley, and then the rock-walled gorge to Portland, is over one hundred miles in length. We saw a couple of large dams, with locks for river navigation, as well as hydro-electric generation stations. These are the same dams that have stopped salmon migration on this huge river. Several small ocean freighters were on the waterway along with Midwest style river towboats pushing barges.

A number of small towns, plus a small city named The Dalles, were on our side of the river. These towns were situated where the riverbank was broad enough to contain buildings and houses, or where a gorge cut through from the high plateau above down to the river. The high vertical rock walls of the actual gorge were immense and extended almost all the way to Portland. After a while, pine trees appeared along the route, and by the time we reached Hood River, pine trees were everywhere, with rock cliffs still rising above. This was the Oregon I had hoped to see. Trees! But don't get me wrong, the brown round hills were impressive as well.

Very few bridges cross the river, but at Biggs Junction, just downriver from John Day Lock & Dam, the gorge was narrow enough to make a bridge feasible. Todd hoped that would mean a convenient gas station would be nearby. It was a good plan, but the confusing ramp signage resulted in us getting off at a town called Rufus, just before Biggs Junction.

There was a gas station, but getting our large RV into it was not all that convenient, but that did not deter him.

Here we encountered one of the quirks one finds while traveling. In Oregon, it is against the law for a customer to pump their own fuel—an attendant has to do it. Todd went to grab the pump and was shooed away by a heavyset, greasy looking guy wearing a dirt-smudged orange safety vest. I was going to clean the windows a bit, in spite of the fact it was drizzling, but could find no squeegees. Then I spotted a bunch of homeless guys, crouched with their backs against the side of the gas station, who had commandeered all the squeegees. Windshields were cleaned for tips. Todd and I briefly discussed what we had experienced. I went inside to use the restroom and get some coffee. When I went to the counter to pay, the clerk asked if we had filled up on fuel, and when I said yes, they said the coffee was free. I like free coffee, but the rest of the stuff would take a bit of getting used to.

We changed drivers after the fuel stop. Todd had been driving non-stop for over four hours and needed a well-deserved break. He looked over at me while I was getting settled into the captain's chair, and said with a chuckle, "Well, partner, I got us in here. Let's see you get us out!"

It was going to be a tricky maneuver since we were right beside the road and facing the opposite direction we wanted to go. Getting clear of the fuel pumps and other cars at the station was the first task, then finding a piece of pavement where I could swing the beast around was the next, but I did it, even though I was blocking the entrance to several nearby businesses. Then, gauging the flow of traffic in both directions for a gap to present itself, I declared, "Clear the deck you sumbitches, I'm coming out!" and swung the yacht across two lanes of traffic and got positioned at the traffic light to make our turn.

"Jesus!" Todd muttered from the passenger seat.

"Hey, we're bigger than everyone else! Sometimes you have to use that to your advantage."

Motoring down through the gorge we gazed at the cliffs and the river. At some spots, heavy clouds were suspended low over the edge of the cliff on the opposite side, which was rather strange looking. The remains of the original gorge road were occasionally visible on our side of the valley, gouged into the rock of the cliff. It looked to be a single lane road. The whole drive along the river to Portland was spectacularly scenic. We were making good time, and the drizzle had become more sporadic.

"We are getting close to Portland. Maybe we should figure out where we are going before we find ourselves right downtown," I said to Todd, as a "Portland 20 miles" sign swept by.

"Where do you want to go? If we stay on this road won't we end up at the ocean?"

"If I recall, from studying the map, I-84 ends in Portland. In order to go to the ocean, we have to get on some other road."

"Do you have a place in mind?" he asked.

"I have no clue! Check the Rand McNally. Once we hit the coast, it looks like there is a state park just about every five miles or so. I have never been here, but my guess is they are all cool, and if not, just go to the next one. You would think there would be RV parks nearby as well."

"I will get on it!"

"Well find something quick! That last sign said Portland is only 20 miles away!"

"Where's Amy live? How about finding something near her, so we do not have so far to drive when we have to drop this thing off?"

"That's a fine idea! She lives in McMinnville, which is southwest of Portland," I replied, "and I also need you to guide me through, or around Portland."

"You mean you do not have all the Interstates memorized by now? I've seen you studying the map a lot!" he said with a laugh.

"Not hardly!" I replied. "I have seen you checking it out a lot too! But when we were getting close to Idaho, I think you were looking at the Hawaii map on the other page!"

Todd started laughing again. "I was! I was planning my trip next week! I have been there before, but now I have found some new places to see."

"Well get us around Portland, or you will not be making it to Hawaii!"

Todd opened the map on the dashboard shelf and started checking his phone as well. "Okay, I found McMinnville. Take I-205 to I-5"

Utilizing modern technology to its fullest extent, Todd searched on his phone for RV parks but was having problems making connections. He continued fiddling around on his phone, then asked, "Hey, I found a place called Pacific City! Do you think it's on the ocean?"

"With a name like that, it is almost a sure bet! And if it isn't, they ought to be sued for false advertising!" Then I added, "I am too busy driving to remember what you just told me, so as we approach the interchanges I am going to ask you again, so don't put the map away."

"I am going to help you out, brother! I put the directions to Pacific City on my phone, and I will link it up to the radio speakers in the RV. The phone will give you the directions." He started messing with wires and plugging them into the jacks by the radio. We were now crawling along in heavy traffic. Welcome to greater metropolitan Portland!

"Will that bitch give me directions in time to do something?"

"Oh, yeah! She will let you know well in advance," Todd replied assuredly.

We had gotten on the I-205 bypass, and the heavy traffic came to a stop, before inching along again. There were warning signs cautioning "road construction ahead" but we never saw any. Nevertheless, traffic crept along. We commented on the fact the Portland drivers seemed more polite about the situation, whereas in Columbus road rage would have been breaking out all over the place. We also noticed the extraordinary number of homeless camps along the highway and under the bridges. They were obvious by the numerous blue plastic tarpaulins stretched over tents and stacks of wooden pallets, but we did not see any people.

"IN TWO MILES, GET OFF ON I-5 SOUTH !!!!!!!!!!" a female voice loudly cooed over the speakers.

"Jesus! She scared me half to death!"

"Is it too loud for ya, Fred?" Todd said while laughing uncontrollably.

"Just a bit! I want to follow the directions, not be freaked out by them!" I replied.

The now lowered voice directed us across a broad valley between the Willamette River and the coastal mountain range. Mixed agriculture, instead of a single crop like hay, was now much in evidence. Nursery plants of trees and bushes, wine vineyards, berries, as well as walnuts and hazelnuts were the primary agri-businesses in this valley. We went around the town of McMinnville, where several buildings housed the Evergreen International Air Museum. One building had a Boeing 747 jumbo jet sitting on its roof.

"You don't see that all the time!" I remarked as we rolled by.

"No, you don't," Todd drolly replied. "So when do we get to the ocean?"

"We have to go through those!" I said, pointing at the windshield toward the mountains, now looming much larger in the distance.

"Christ! More mountains?"

"Yup! But those should be the last ones. The coast should be just beyond that," I said, trying to reassure him that we could not be too far now.

We had been talking some more when I heard the female voice say something but could not hear it. "Oh, crap! She said something, but I missed it!"

"Don't worry! She will repeat it when we get closer," Todd replied while staring at something out the side window.

"IN 500 FEET, TURN RIGHT ON ROUTE 22," the soothing voice commanded from the overhead speakers.

"I don't see a road up there, can you?"
"There it is! By that barn! Where the pickup truck pulling the trailer just turned!" Todd said while pointing energetically toward the right of the windshield.
"Shit! That was not much warning, and I still do not see a route marker!" I said while hitting the turn signal, mashing on the brakes, and making the sharp turn like I knew what I was doing, instead of like a lost tourist.

The route turned out to be a narrow, extremely twisty two-lane road. I was glad the pickup truck pulling a trailer of building supplies was up ahead of us because he could not go too fast. Occasionally he would get up to 40 mph, but mostly we wound around and up through hills and forest at about 25 miles an hour. The mountains of the coastal range rise above 3,000 feet and are covered by dense pine forest, which is cut through by deep ravines and gullies. There was no guardrail or wire along the edge of the road, in fact in most places there was no berm either, and there were very few houses. After following the pickup with the trailer, for ten or fifteen minutes, I was getting used to how he was handling the road. Then he slowed down and pulled off to go down a short drive to a little house. I was now on my own. However, we really were not alone because looking in the sideview mirrors revealed about seven or eight vehicles following closely behind the RV, and we were now the lead vehicle.

At some mysterious point, the road entered a zone of rain forest. The tall pines were cloaked with a thick drapery of green moss, as were fallen logs and large rocks. Huge feathery green ferns erupted from the lush, inclined landscape. I did my best to focus on the road, but the sight of this riot of green growth made that difficult. Occasionally we could glimpse a boulder-filled stream at the bottom of a ravine, but mostly the drop-offs were too steep, and filled with trees and ferns to see the bottom. All I could do was take quick looks and steer through the curves, and up and down, while the RV rocked back and forth. I doubt the traffic backing up behind us took much comfort from the sight of a slow-moving giant mobile home swaying back and forth while swooping around curves.

At one point, when the RV was really rocking, I took my hands off the wheel and yelled, "Yee haw! Ride'm cowboy!" and then resumed my steering duties.

Todd made no comment during any of this, but I noted he had been hanging on to the cup rail beside him and was keenly observing the ravines dropping away below his side window. I got the impression he was about as nervous as I had been when he was driving in Yellowstone, while peeling tinfoil off his chocolates. That was not my intent, but I was now confident in how the vehicle handled on this particular road, so I felt good and was having fun.

A short patch of pull off pavement materialized around a sharp bend, but we were going too fast to utilize it. I made a mental note that at the next one I would pull off to let the traffic go by. Sure enough, in a couple of miles another pull off came up, with just enough space to accommodate the Land Yacht, and I was able to get off the road. I took the tooting of horns as the cars and trucks sped by to be signals of appreciation. They could just as well been signifiers of exasperation, but I saw no middle fingers come out any windows, so notes of courtesy will remain my interpretation.

Driving on such a winding road in thick forest, it was hard to tell where we were. For quite a while the uphill climbs outnumbered the downhills, and then at some point we must have crossed a summit and downhills predominated. There was another rainforest zone, and the road started to follow a very picturesque rocky stream. Too bad I was driving, and too bad there was no place to pull off for a while, because I would have loved to have taken some pictures. Two old single-lane iron truss bridges, several miles apart, crossed the widening stream. Just before the first bridge, there was another pull off, which allowed me to once again discharge another accretion of vehicles from our rear. The second bridge turned out to be at the lower edge of the mountain range. After crossing it, the road leveled out and followed the stream out of the thinning forest. We passed a white diamond sign with a blue curling wave, stating "TSUNAMI ZONE!"

"We are close now, Todd!" I shouted with excitement. "If we are in the tsunami zone, then we are near the ocean!" However, the notification was a rather disquieting bit of information, for it meant that without warning a giant wave could reach this far inland and kill us.

The next several bends in the road left the forest behind and wound along the edge of tidal salt marshes. Ahead in the distance, above the marshes and trees, stood the hazy silhouette of a great rock.

"Todd, that rock is at the ocean! Before we go anywhere else, I would like to try to get where we can look at it!"

"Sounds good to me!" Todd was now exhibiting greater interest in our proximity to saltwater.

Our road came to an end at US-101, the famed Pacific Coast Highway. The female voice was talking, but I was ignoring her because I was trying to figure out the next turn to get to the large rock. I turned right and planned to take the next left I could find.

"IN A QUARTER MILE, TURN LEFT ON BROOTEN ROAD TO PACIFIC CITY," the voice cooed.

"We are here! And she is taking us to the rock! How cool is that?!" I shouted, not able to contain my excitement.

Open water by the marshes, but not the ocean, was visible from the narrow road that skirted along the wooded shore. Pacific City turned out to be a long, small town situated on a spit of land between a sizable protected lagoon and the shorefront sand dunes. The road crossed a small bridge over the lagoon. The area by the bridge served as the main business district, with pizza shops and restaurants, two marijuana dispensaries, a hardware store, sports store, and a couple of bars, along with various boat and marina type concerns. There were no signs, and the rock was now obscured by a high line of sand dunes ahead of us. I had no idea where I was going until I spotted a small sign pointing left to a boat ramp. Hoping the boat ramp would be near the ocean, I turned in the direction the sign indicated. The narrow road, with pavement that was crumbling away into the sand on either side, was actually a residential street. It was barely wide enough for cars to pass each other, while avoiding vehicles parked in front of the homes lining the street, so our vehicle was much larger than what the street was ever designed for. Some houses were new, but most appeared to have been built in the late 1950s or 1960s, originally as vacation beach houses. I was trying my best to navigate our thirty-seven-foot motor home down this morass of obstructions, when suddenly, BANG!!

"Watch your clearance," Todd dryly observed, as I scraped through some stout scraggly pine trees.

"Damn! I hope I didn't rip the air conditioning units off the roof!" I replied, fearing the worst. "That certainly did not sound good!"

Spying another "park" sign pointing left, we soon found ourselves on a large, paved lot for boat launching and parking, facing the lagoon. The view across the small bay was of hills covered with pine trees and houses scattered across them. To the south, the mountains of the Pacific Coast Range could be seen in the distance. A few small boats with fishermen cruised in the large lagoon.

"I don't think this is the ocean," Todd stated flatly.

"I don't think so either, but there is a public restroom, which I definitely could use, and we can check to see how badly I tore up Amy's RV," I replied while finding a place to park.

Pine needles were stuck in the arm of the roll-up canopy on the side, but all the equipment on the roof appeared to have not been damaged at all. Disaster averted! We were very relieved. I went over to some fishermen, who were unloading their gear out of an old beat-up Nissan pickup truck, and asked if there was another park nearby where we could see the rock. They said there was, and it was on down the road, but would provide no directions.

A bit miffed by the lack of helpful assistance for a lost tourist, I walked back to Todd and announced, "We are close! There is another park, but those guys really did not care about providing any more info other than 'it is down the road.'"

"Well, let's go down the road then," Todd happily declared.

Decisions, decisions. I decided to turn left and continue on down the street, which soon ended in a small parking lot full of vehicles. A small sign stated, "Robert Straub State Park." Fortunately, I found a place to park. The lot was on the edge of a line of high white sand dunes covered with seagrass.

"Where is the ocean?" Todd asked with obvious disappointment.

"On the other side of those dunes. Go over them, and you will be looking at the Pacific Ocean! We made it, Todd!" I replied with a sense of accomplishment and satisfaction, then started getting my camera stuff together. Todd just sat in the passenger seat looking at the dunes in deep contemplation. I never saw him that still, so I took a picture of him.

Day 7 *Todd sits in contemplation. The Pacific Ocean is just over the sand dune to the right.*
Robert Straub State Park, Pacific City, Oregon.

There was a path of sorts, from the parking lot into the sea grass, and then up into the dunes. A fairly stiff breeze rustled the grass, but that sound was soon drowned out by thundering surf. Cresting the dune revealed a magnificent panorama of the Pacific Ocean. Huge waves, 8 to 10 feet high, rolled in to crash on the beach shoreline about five hundred feet away. To the south, the land, maybe a mile away, curved out further into the sea, and the view was hazy from the salt spray in the air. Looking north was the huge rock we had seen earlier. It appeared to be a couple of miles up the coast, and maybe a mile out in the ocean. The rock just erupted up several hundred feet out of the water, with no other similar feature to be seen. It was stunning in its solitude.

Sea grass on the sand dune, an expansive beach, and haze from the crashing surf of the Pacific Ocean. Robert Straub State Park, Pacific City, Oregon.

Just over the crest of the dune, a bunch of young folks were preparing for a serious beach party. A pickup truck sunk to its axles in the sand was accompanied by a stack of coolers, a gas grill, and hay bales. The merry band was getting the party organized while yelling encouragement and instructions to the pickup truck driver as he proceeded to spin the wheels deeper into the sand. Presently, another truck arrived to pull him out. During our time on the coast, we would witness this process a number of more times, with varying degrees of success.

The beach was very clean, right down to the surf line. It lacked seashells, much to my disappointment. The sand extended for miles in both directions, and there was a scattering of people enjoying the sunny day, in spite of the cold stiff breeze. We talked to a couple, about our age, sitting on blankets and taking in the view and activity just like we were. They were from Portland and came to Pacific City on a regular basis. They informed us that the rock was called Haystack Rock, and that there were some okay places to eat in the area, and a lot more places to get good beer and decent wine. The brief story of our trip, and how we happened upon this beach interested them, especially the fact we had no plan to arrive at this particular place. It was agreed that fate had served us well.

Watching the mesmerizing heavy surf of the Pacific Ocean, at the Robert Straub State Park in Pacific City, Oregon.

My traveling companion, Todd, on the beach. Haystack Rock rising out of the ocean several miles away. Pacific City, Oregon.

Much as we would have liked to hang out on the beach for hours, we decided we ought to try to find a suitable RV park for the night, so we bid adieu to the friendly couple. Trudging back up the high dune and through the tall grass toward the mobile home we managed to get lost enough to exit the natural maze at the far end of the parking lot from where we parked. Todd and I were giddy with excitement at the prospect of being near the ocean for the next day or so. There was no discussion, just big smiles as I drove back up the so-called street.

"You know, Fred," Todd said at last, "you really impressed me back there."

"Where?"

"On that road over those last mountains. That took some real driving. I wasn't sure you had it in ya, but you did!"

"Thanks, but I really did not have a choice once we got on that road."

"No, I'm serious."

"I know you are, and I thank you for the compliment. Coming from you, a professional driver, I truly appreciate it!"

"You would make a good school bus driver."

"Not really!"

"No, you would. Seriously!"

"I might be able to handle a bus," I replied in all earnestness, "but I do not think I could handle the kids, so I would not make a good school bus driver. I would probably wind up choking half of them!"

"Well, it is something to consider," was Todd's parting advice.

The lack of directional or information signs meant we had to make choices at the intersection before the lagoon bridge. I turned left, in the direction of the rock. About half a mile up what turned out to be a secondary coastal road, we came into another small business area of Pacific City. There were surf and trinket shops, along with art galleries and small restaurants, all of which appeared to be closed for the season. A sign declaring the entrance to "Cape Kiwanda RV Resort" caught Todd's attention.

"Right there!" Todd declared, "Pull in and let's see if they are open, and have any spaces!"

As we pulled into one of the designated parking zones for check-in and looked at the guardhouse by a nice tall black metal fence, and the large park office complex to the side, we knew this was a whole new level of RV park. Exiting the land yacht to walk over to the office, I looked across the street and stopped in my tracks.

"Hey, Todd! Check it out!" I said while pointing in the direction of the ocean, "We are right across the street from Haystack Rock! I can't believe it!"

"I think we done good! Let's just hope they have a space!" Todd replied with a big grin.

"They won't have a space for the likes of us if you keep talking like a hick!" I said, and we were both laughing all the way to the office door.

The office took up a small area by the side door of a much larger building facing the street, the ocean, and Haystack Rock. Also in the building was a large section of tourist type stuff like beach shoes and clothing, books, and post cards. Beyond that was a full seafood delicatessen and ice cream shop, then a small grocery store for use by the locals and walk-in visitors from the street, as well as guests of the RV park. The 'resort' clerk said there was space, and informed us that full hookups were available along with several laundry and shower buildings, plus an indoor swimming pool, and a small exercise room. The rate was $57 per night, which was the highest rate so far on this trip but considering the amenities, and the to-die-for location, quite a bargain.

We rolled past the gate toward our assigned spot, passing happy people on lawn chairs and at picnic tables by campfire rings, relaxing by their motor homes and campers. Trees were by each lot and was all surrounded by well-trimmed green grass. One group had several very large rabbits hopping around, which I thought strange, but since we were in Oregon, maybe rabbits were the new cool pet to have. As we found out later, there was a whole herd of rabbits hired by this resort to keep the grass cut. They did a fine job and did not get rowdy, make any noise, or emit smoke.

As I swung into our space, I remarked to Todd that it appeared we had one of the largest motor homes here. On our journey I had been comparing ours to others, and while some were the same size or a bit larger, they were not as numerous. Much larger motor homes do exist, but they cost upwards of a million dollars. Thus it dawned on me a whole new appreciation for what we had been entrusted to drive across the country. I also had an appreciation for how classy of a joint this was to spend the night. Based on limited experience, I thought the place in Cody, Wyoming was probably about as good as it could get, but I was wrong.

The hookup process went smoothly, as did extending the sliders. There was nothing left to do but to go out and explore. I decided to wander around the 'resort' park so I would be familiar with the roads, paths, and location of the shower house, laundry, and trash bins. Plus, I wanted to check out the tourist store up front. Turns out there was a lot of stuff to see, and purchase, but I limited myself to postcards and a Pacific City sweatshirt.

Cape Kiwanda RV Resort, Pacific City, Oregon. Rabbit-trimmed grass, and Haystack Rock in the distance. Pacific surf could be heard in the background.

Todd was elsewhere when I returned to our RV, and it was locked. I had forgotten to grab my keys on my way out. "Oh, well," I thought, "he will be back soon because I saw him in the store not long ago." There were a couple of empty spaces in front of our RV, and they were in the sun, so I sat on the picnic table and waited. After a couple of cigarettes, and a brief call from Amy, I realized he was not coming back anytime soon, so I gave him a call. At least I had my phone and camera with me.

"Hey, Todd, where ya at?"

"I am on the beach, waiting for the sun to set behind the rock. Where are you?"

"I am sitting outside the RV. I forgot my keys!"

"What did you do that for? Ya want me to come get you?"

"Nope! I will meet you on the beach!" I said, thinking he was in a much better location than I was. The beach is where I had intended to go anyway, after dropping off my tourist swag.

The beach at Pacific City, with the view of Haystack Rock straight out in the ocean, plus Cape Kiwanda jutting out about a quarter of a mile into the water to the north, was impressive. Lots of people were on the beach either walking around or just sitting on the sand enjoying the view. The wind was rather strong, and the temperature was dropping, so it was rather chilly, but the view was too stunning to be deterred by a "fresh breeze," as the British would say. The wind swept the tops off the waves as they broke, and back out toward the sea in veils of exploding spray. Young men in wet suits were surfing the big curling waves. Another pickup truck was stuck in the sand, and a loud old Ford tow truck arrived to winch him out. A wad of cash exchanged hands before that process commenced. I found Todd down by the wave line, watching the sun slowly descending toward Haystack Rock. He was also keeping an eye on the noisy tow truck winching operation.

The sun setting behind Haystack Rock was a stunning sight. We were perfectly located to be able to walk into the long shadow it cast on the beach. It was like being able to control a total solar eclipse by where one stood or moved. I took a lot of pictures, hoping to fully capture the mesmerizing effect. Scores of people were on the beach and the dune watching the evening spectacle. Satisfied we had seen enough, we turned to head up the dune above the beach and search the town for something to eat.

Haystack Rock, Pacific City, Oregon.

Windblown surf at Cape Kiwanda, Pacific City, Oregon in the evening. Surfer done riding for the day.

Setting sun over Haystack Rock.

Setting sun behind Haystack Rock, which is about a mile off the shore, and rises 327 feet out of the ocean.

Pelican Brewery & Pub sits at the top of the dune, with a perfect view of the ocean and Haystack Rock. Their patio was packed with diners and drinkers taking in the view. This place was diagonally across the street from our RV park, so it was a no brainer to stop there for supper. As it turned out, there was an hour and a half wait for a table. We had not eaten since leaving Idaho early in the morning, and any delay was an undue burden to inflict upon two famished travelers such as ourselves. Next choice was the seafood deli in the market at the Cape Kiwanda RV Resort. Todd ordered a big chunk of smoked salmon and some oysters. I asked for the cheap fish & chips, but they were out of plain old whitefish, and only had fresh Halibut, so sparing no expense, that is what I ordered. At this point, I did not care what it cost, as long as it was food. It was the best fish and chips I have ever eaten. The fish melted in my mouth, and the batter on both the fish and the chips had a great, yet unidentifiable seasoning. We ate our food back in the warm comfort of our RV. What a way to top off a fantastic day!

There had been little communication of substance with Amy. I texted her the morning we were in the Black Hills about considering staying put due to the high wind advisory, and that was a day after she had texted Todd that she did not have an available space to park the RV near her home until Monday. After that, she had no idea where we were until today, when Todd sent a photo of the Pacific Ocean and the message, "Guess where we are?" A couple of hours later she called him back for specifics, but he was vague about our location, other than the fact we were on the Oregon coast, that I had locked myself out of the RV, and that he suspected I was writing a book. Later in the evening, I called Amy to update her on our actual whereabouts, and to get specifics regarding the RV delivery. She had arranged a spot at an RV park in McMinnville, but it would not be open until noon on Monday. I told her she should text the address to Todd, and we could use the mapping and direction feature on his smartphone to make the Monday appointment.

We did not have to drive anywhere tomorrow, and that was a first. Being quite satisfied with our present location, we made the decision to stay right where we were until Monday. That also meant we did not have to worry about going to bed, so Todd and I talked for a while, mostly about politics and society. We also discussed the recovery program of Alcoholics Anonymous and God's grace in our lives, both in sobriety in general and specifically in relation to this trip. The places we had been, how we got to most of those places with no plan in mind, and even the weather, all felt like it was way beyond coincidence in how it happened, and that the guidance and presence of a Higher Power had been involved, and strongly felt.

It was an enjoyable conversation, but soon the long day began to take its toll. Todd retired to the back bedroom to make some calls and to watch television. I worked on my journal, for there was a lot of stuff to catch up on while it was still fresh, and I was more than a day behind. An hour of writing was about all I could do before fatigue made it too difficult. Having no pressing agenda looming over me and knowing there was always tomorrow to get current on the writing, I went outside for a bit to enjoy the solitude. The sky was clear and the lights in the area were minimal, so I could see the Milky Way. This fact just amazed me on this trip, because there is so much light pollution in central Ohio that our galaxy is visible only when one is at least fifty miles, or more, outside the Columbus metro area. Another impressive feature was that I could hear the pounding of the surf, which was over a quarter of a mile away. The whole effect of surf and stars re-enforced an all-encompassing sense of peace and serenity.

RV odometer reading: 48,285 miles
Miles driven from Circleville / Lithopolis OH to Pacific City OR <u>3,138 miles</u>
(not including at least 300 + miles driven in Yellowstone in the rental car) **7 days on the road**

Chapter 11
Oregon Rain

Sunday, October 7 -Day 8

New day, and no destination. I got up around 6 AM and headed to the shower house, making sure I had the combination to punch into the keypad to unlock the door. Classy joints like this have everything locked to keep the riffraff out, but all the paying clients have the same code. The temperature felt like it was in the 40s and it was damp outside. Fortunately, the wind had stopped so the walk was tolerable.

After the shower and shave, I called Tammy while sitting on a rock drinking coffee and having a smoke. I told her how cool the place was where we were staying, and that I could hear the pounding of the surf in the background while we were talking. But she was having none of this happy talk, even though I started the conversation by asking how she was and whether she had coughed up any more blood. The quick version went something like this:

"I don't want to hear about how much fun you are having. You were supposed to drive that thing out there, deliver it, and come home. You and Todd turned it into a joy ride!"

"Heck yeah! Why not? The opportunity presented itself. You even agreed!"

"Not to this. I am having a terrible time!"

"I cannot help that."

"Fuck you!"

"If a bunch of your girlfriends offered you a chance to travel, I would be happy for you, and tell you to go," I replied, in the vain hope it would raise the level of discourse a bit.

"I would not go!"

"That makes no sense! You were for the idea of me going, until you weren't. And if the same opportunity was offered to you, you would not go?"

"I would not! I would not do to you what you are doing to me!"

"What are you talking about?!"

"It was going to be one thing, then you were not going, then it becomes this great trip, and you left me all alone!"

"You are acting like a child!" That was the conversation killer. There was no point arguing, and I said so, and then said goodbye.

A light rain had started fall. It made no sense to be sitting in the rain while my wife yelled at me long distance from two thousand miles away. We have choices in life, and at that moment I chose not to listen to any more insanity. However, sitting on a rock in a light rain while surf crashed in the distance now seemed to be a fine option after I put my phone back in my pocket. I reveled in the solitude of the moment and lit another cigarette.

The rain got heavier and steady as the morning wore on. Todd was definitely sleeping in. After my normal Raisin Bran cereal breakfast, I set up shop in the passenger seat to write in my journal. It was a good location since there was a tray that pulled out of the RV dashboard, upon which I could write and scrutinize maps and leaflets that I had collected along the way. I could also look out the window and daydream. There is a record album by Australian musician, Cortney Barnett, with the title, *Sometimes I sit and think. Sometimes, I just sit*. That was a rather apt summation as to what was going on in the passenger seat of the RV on this cold, damp morning, and I was fine with it. After the over-stimulation of the past week, I needed the time to unwind and reflect.

There were no great epiphanies. It was more like meditation. I was is sitting in the best loge seat in a theater, and a one-act play of life, from the resort park perspective, was unfolding in front of me. Low clouds were draped over the forested hill overlooking the RV park. The residents were out and about, heading to the beach to go surfing, or going to the shower house. Most were in flip-flops and shorts but acknowledged the rain and cold by wearing stout looking name-brand outdoor-outfitter ponchos and windbreakers. Most fascinating were the rabbits going about their business of keeping the grass trimmed. They seemed well suited for the weather and were not bothered one bit. A truly relaxing experience, and I was immensely enjoying just sitting and watching. Being on the coastal Pacific Northwest, which I understand has a lot of rain, I decided that I too would get up and go about once I completed my writing assignment, and not let the wet deter me. Such are the 'big' decisions one makes when life slows down to simply the moment at hand.

Day 8 Clouds hugging the mountain, and steady rain— the view from my writer's spot in our RV at Cape Kiwanda RV Resort in Pacific City, Oregon

The previous night, while we were having our leisurely chat, Todd revealed that he had brought a firearm along for the trip. He thought it might come in handy if we encountered any desperadoes on the highway. I said that I would have liked to have known that so I could have gotten down low in the event he was forced to commence pumping lead through the walls at any evil doers. That was an advantage of being in a thin-skinned mobile home—no aim required. I could have avoided becoming collateral damage had I known about the weaponry beforehand. He said he was not sure how I would react to news of armament on board because guns are a touchy subject with most people. Now he was confronted with the problem of how to get the gun back home. Todd had not planned on checking his bags through the airport when getting on the airplane for the return flight home. He was going to do carry-on instead. I tried to ease his fears by telling him he could take the gun, but it would have to be in his luggage and would have to be checked in. Carry-on with weaponry was out of the question. He had hoped that he could put the gun in one of the bags that I had planned to check, but I said that I would not be comfortable with that, and it was probably illegal anyway. Since he had as much crap as I did, if not more, he would be forced to check at least one bag through, because the airline would not permit that many bags to be considered as all carry-on. And finally, I suggested he check with the TSA website to learn their requirements, for this would not be the first time someone had encountered the same issue. That ended that line of conversation for the evening.

    Still hard at work at the task of writing in my journal, and looking out the window at the fog, rain, and rabbits, Todd materialized from the back of the RV and announced he was going to walk downtown to the hardware store to get a case for his gun, as specified on the TSA website. He took the umbrella and was gone.

    My daydreaming and writing took up most of the morning, but I finally got that completed, along with consuming multiple cups of coffee and cigarettes. While wandering around inside the RV, working up the fortitude to go outside and do something productive, I found the information packet and brochure from the Kiwanda RV Resort and started reading. I am easily distracted. It had interesting factoids about the town of Pacific City, Haystack Rock, and the local fishing industry. It also had a number of warnings for folks unfamiliar to the area, such as "be on alert for earthquakes" and "watch out for tsunamis," which may or may not be preceded by a warning. It did not say what form that warning may take, so the assumption was that it would be obvious. That was not very comforting, nor was the advice to run to higher ground "without delay!" Another warning was that of "sneaker waves." Apparently, a lot of times every seventh or ninth wave of surf is bigger than the others, and they have a tendency to "sneak up" on people not paying attention. The result is that the wave knocks them over and drags them out to sea. The best advice was to not turn your back to the ocean.

When I was a child, our family took annual summer trips to New England, and my brother and I had noticed this phenomenon a number of times during visits to the shore. These childhood memories had long been buried by other trivia, so the warning in the brochure was an excellent reminder. My reading of the brochure continued to other dangers, like sharks and whales, and I was beginning to ponder the multitude of things in this idyllic spot that could result in one's untimely demise, when Todd stumbled back through the door looking disheveled, exhausted, and wet.

It turned out the hardware store was about a mile away, down by the bridge over the lagoon, and there was no sidewalk, so he either had to walk in wet sand or on the road. The wind had picked up and did a number on the umbrella which severely compromised its water repellent abilities. To make matters worse, the hardware did not stock gun carry-on cases. But the trip was not a total loss. Two marijuana dispensaries were located in that vicinity, so Todd decided to check one out. Ohio had recently passed a medical marijuana law, but implementation of a distribution system was slow and did not yet exist. Oregon, however, had passed a recreational marijuana law making the purchase of weed in a variety of forms completely legal, if said purchase was from a licensed dispensary. He said the storefront operation was nice, with a friendly and very stoned clerk ready to answer any questions about edibles, smokables, oils, and other forms of cannabis. Todd purchased a pre-rolled joint for five dollars. It came in a clear plastic tube with a brand name on the black and white label which also stated the name of the dispensary, location, THC content of 22%, and several bar-codes, along with the producer's name and city. He popped the cap off the tube and dumped the joint on the table. I picked it up and inhaled its pungent aroma, as one might take in the smell of a fine cigar before firing it up.

"Whoa! This is the good shit!" I declared with a smile. I knew that was true without a doubt. During my years before sobriety, I considered myself quite the connoisseur of the various strains and traits of the ganja. The aroma was that of potent sinsemilla bud, and I recognized it immediately even after more than thirty years of being away from it.

"You think?" Todd replied with glee.

"So, what are you going to do with it?" I inquired.

"Does it make you uncomfortable?" he probed.

"A little bit. How about you?"

"Yeah, kinda," he replied thoughtfully.

"So why did you get it?"

"I could not believe I could actually walk into a store and buy pot. So, I did! I will throw it away if it is making you squirrelly, but I knew you would be interested and want to see it!"

"You are so thoughtful, Todd! And yes I am glad you showed it to me, but throwing it away is rather drastic! Give it away to somebody."

"I was thinking the same thing," he concluded.

Todd was chilly and wet, so he said he was going to change clothes, dry the wet stuff, and get something warm to drink. I had been in the RV long enough and headed out, first to get a rain poncho at the market and pay the park fee for the next day, then check out the beach. He offered the battered umbrella, which I accepted, but after seeing its condition, I had already concluded I would need some extra coverage.

It was definitely a gray and dismal day on the beach, with wind and rain showers, but that did not stop the surfers from giving the waves a try. They were going to get wet anyway, so the weather made little difference. It appeared to be about high tide and the waves were quite large. I was taking pictures of

Haystack Rock in the fog when a "sneaker wave" came rolling in and chased me about one hundred feet up the beach, much to my chagrin. I had been trying to put my camera back in the bag while shielding it from the rain, and in the process had turned my back to the surf, just like the brochure had warned me from doing.

Windblown surf breaking on the Pacific City, Oregon beach. Haystack Rock looms beyond a lone surfer.

Lousy weather not deterring a surfer from catching a curl in the distance. Decent rain gear was a must for walking on the beach, while the surfers stay relatively warm in wet suits. Nestucca Bay at Pacific City, Oregon.

Wandering around outside in this weather seemed rather pointless, so I headed back to the RV and arrived in time to join Todd for a late lunch of Manwhich® that he had just cooked. That hit the spot. The rain and fog continued all day, and the temperature hovered around 55°, so after lunch, we started watching cable TV. One of the cable channels was having an *American Pickers* marathon, or maybe that is the standard viewing fair for rainy Sunday afternoons. That show was better than any of the other dismal offerings. We both fell asleep after one episode. This was the first downtime we experienced following a whole week of non-stop driving, and we both needed a day of rest even though we would not have admitted it. Had there been some destination, or simply more miles to go, we would have been alert and rolling.

Rousing from our lethargy late in the afternoon, we got some coffee, then stumbled around the mobile home tidying up and doing a preliminary cleaning of the floors, etc. It was not that the place had been trashed, but it had been lived in for a week. Although we did not realize it at the time we started this trek, but we are both clean and neat freaks to a certain extent and were quite compatible in that regard. That flurry of activity was taxing, so we declared the job was sufficiently complete for the moment and it was an appropriate hour to go out for supper.

The Pelican Brew House, being right across the street from our resort park and the fact it was open, made it an obvious choice, so that is where we went. The crappy weather eliminated the fair-sky tourists, so the place was not packed like the night before when there was a great view from the floor to ceiling windows, and patio, of the setting sun. Nevertheless, Haystack Rock, the surf and ocean, plus the huge dune that comprises Cape Kiwanda, are all appealing to look at even in the fog and blowing drizzle, and especially from the warm side of heavy plate-glass. The waiter was friendly, jovial, and efficient, and was probably in his early forties, so he was the oldest server in the room. He also lacked the piercings and tattoos of his young hipster cohort, which made him stand out even more.

"Good evening, gentlemen, my name is Shawn, and I will be your server tonight. Where are you from?"

"What? I thought you were going to ask us what we wanted to drink, first. What makes you think we ain't from around here?" Todd replied sarcastically, with a quizzical smile.

"Yeah! Do we have 'tourist' written all over our faces?" I asked with mock indignation, then added, "Where are *you* from?"

Shawn chuckled and was obviously game for our antics. "I like to establish rapport with my customers, and I like to know where they are from because we get people in here from all over. In fact, I keep track of where people come from!" With that, he flipped over his clipboard to reveal a map with states colored in and country names along the edges.

"Impressive! At first, I thought you might be an undercover Homeland Security agent. Have you had anybody from Ohio yet?" I replied.

"You are the second ones today!" Shawn replied, then added, "O – H!," expecting the Pavlovian

Buckeye response of 'I – O!' and high-five hand slaps in praise of the Ohio State football team.

"Good, God!" snorted Todd while shaking his head in dismay, "You can't get away from them!"

"So, you guys are not fans?" Shawn responded in astonishment. "I thought everyone from Ohio was!"

"Nope! We are not part of that mass psychosis! Admittedly, that puts us in the minority," I replied. "By the way, do you live here in Pacific City?"

"No, I live in Lincoln City," Shawn replied, almost apologetically. "Hard to live here on a server's wage."

"Oh, so you live down the coast. Is it cheaper there?" I asked.

"A little bit. Especially if you already own your house. Are you familiar with Lincoln City?"

"Not at all! I study maps, so I have a general idea where it is. Does Lincoln City have a big rock sitting out in the ocean?" I replied. Shawn looked at me quizzically.

"He really does look at maps—all the time!" Todd interjected in feigned disgust while perusing the menu.

"Actually, there are only three places along the Oregon coast that have these rock formations. This is one of them, but Lincoln City does not. The better-known rock, which is also called Haystack Rock, is about eighty miles up the coast at Cannon Beach. Everybody thinks they are everywhere, but they aren't."

"Really?!" I was incredulous. "I thought big rocks on the coast were part of the whole Oregon experience!"

"That is the impression! Now don't get me wrong, all of the coast is very scenic; stunning, actually. Is that what brought you to Pacific City?"

"Sort of, but not really," Todd responded with an air of mystery. Then to somewhat resolve the mystery, added, "We are delivering an RV from Ohio to McMinnville for a friend and we ended up here."

Shawn grimaced in consternation, then laughed. "Well, I think you overshot McMinnville! In fact, you may have gone through it!"

"We did!" Todd declared with satisfaction, still examining the bill of fare.

"We had no clue what was here until we arrived!" I stated proudly. "He liked the name," I added, nodding in Todd's direction.

"Lucky! And great choice!"

"Yeah, that is how this whole trip across the country has been! It's been great!" I replied while taking a glance at the glossy photos of food on the menu.

"So, what will you have to drink, and would you like to start off with one of our signature appetizers?" Shawn said, returning to the business at hand.

The up-scale American sit-down restaurant cheeseburgers we ordered, with exotic leafy vegetable matter that bore little resemblance to the iceberg lettuce us Midwesterners are used to, on a bun the likes of which is not regularly encountered in normal daily activity, was accompanied by a vast quantity of huge French fries. The meal was sufficient in volume to feed a small village in Ethiopia, and it was excellent. Most of the food I had during this trip had been excellent so far, and possibly quite normal. However, I had the feeling we had really lucked out, especially in Oregon, though my basis for comparison is limited. I have had fine meals in a number of places over the years. Back at home, Tammy and I rarely eat out, and when we do treat ourselves to a restaurant meal, it is at the Marcy Diner, several miles down the road from Lithopolis, and located in an old general store building, or we go to a Waffle House if there is not a local 'greasy spoon' evident when we are on the road. While culinary adventurism is not my thing, I do recognize and enjoy above-average food when I get it. Numerous business trips to Chicago, and other cities around the country, have expanded my epicurean knowledge and pleasure—paid for on the company's dime. At home, we simply cannot afford fine dining, or to eat out anywhere on a regular basis, so these few meals had been quite a treat.

Following this enjoyable repast, we walked out on the dune above the beach to take a final look at the steel grey surf with the looming rock sentinel out in the mist. There were still a few stalwart individuals down by the water's edge enjoying the scene in spite of the weather, but the numbers had vastly diminished from earlier in the day, and nothing like the fair-weather throng the previous evening to witness the setting sun. We took some more pictures, then headed back to the RV to get out of the cold rain.

Conversation in the comfort of our warm 'home away from home' transitioned into mindless viewing of a movie on cable TV titled *Batman V Superman: Dawn of Justice*. It was just as stupid as the name implied, and after about an hour of this drivel, it was patently obvious it was not going to improve. In fact, it had gotten worse. I declared that I could not take any more mind-numbing crap, nor was I remotely interested in seeing if something better might be on because it was highly likely this was the best cable television had to offer on this particular evening. Todd dejectedly got up and shuffled back to his secluded sanctuary in the back of the RV. I went to bed.

Chapter 12
The Real World

Monday, October 8-Day 9

My internal alarm clock got me up around 6 AM, as usual, and the light rain and fog were still present, but it did seem a bit warmer than yesterday. Went to the shower house and my phone went off twice while I was bathing and shaving. It was Tammy, so I called her back after I returned to the RV and got some coffee. She sounded better than she had for the past several days—less anger. I asked her what had changed, and she said she no longer was afraid that she had been replaced by travel and Todd, and while still not entirely thrilled about my absence, she assured me she would pick me up at the airport upon my return.

Todd must have been exhausted by our rigorous day yesterday and slept in late again. For the second day in a row, there was no pressing reason to get up early. However, I am an early riser by nature and find it rather nice to take advantage of the solitary time created by those who are not. I had my usual RV trip breakfast of raisin bran cereal, then another cup of coffee and a smoke while sitting up front in my lair watching the rain, the fog rolling over the hill, and the rabbits hopping around the park just like yesterday. The weekend trippers all cleared out yesterday because they had to be back at work today. Me? Well, I did not have to be anywhere until noon. I could hear the surf thudding in the background, and the alto moan of a small foghorn over in the lagoon. It was very serene and peaceful. I would take this over the roar and rumble of traffic I hear at home any day.

My reverie was disrupted by my phone ringing. It was Tammy, and she was now in a total funk and depressed. This was a quick turn of emotion, but when living with a person who is bi-polar, not especially unusual. I did my best to convince her that we are okay, and not to obsess about our relationship not being okay. Over the years I have come to understand that it is impossible to dissuade her from whatever idea has overtaken her consciousness. The thought, or emotion, or idea, gives no ground to logic, so I may as well be pissing into the wind. It just gets messy, but I try anyway out of love and empathy. Whether across the kitchen table or across thousands of miles on the telephone, the process is the same. Comfort and reassurance, plus the reminder that "this too, shall pass." Talking her back from the brink, if only for a moment, is about as much success that I can hope for. The rest is her own internal process. It is exhausting for both of us.

Todd got up and downed a cup of coffee. There was no point hanging around this idyllic place any longer, so we disconnected everything, stowing it all in the side compartments, and had the RV rolling by 9 AM. Exiting Kiwanda RV Resort Park, we looked out to the ocean one last time. Fog obscured everything, including Haystack Rock.

"Well, Todd, say goodbye to Pacific City! It sure was nice!" I said as I cranked on the steering wheel and headed down the street.

"Sure was! Looks like a good time to leave though, because you can't see anything anyhow!" Todd declared while giving a slow wave to nothing in particular out the window.

The vague plan was to get back on US-101 and head south to RT-18 near Lincoln City, then go east to McMinnville, while stopping at any parks along the way to see what we could see. The light rain and fog, plus the completely obscured view of Haystack Rock we had just experienced, indicated to us that there would be a change in that plan. Any vistas we had hoped to encounter were now wishful thinking. Road markers to beaches and scenic views taunted us. To go down those side roads was pointless, so I kept driving. We did get to see some very huge trees growing along the road that had miraculously escaped the woodman's saw, and I would have stopped so we could pay our respects and marvel properly, but I was too busy driving. Besides, this vehicle did not lend itself to whipping off to the side of the road on a whim. Nevertheless, I was thrilled to see some trees with trunks that appeared to be at least ten feet in diameter, projecting majestically up from the roadside into the mass of green of the surrounding forest. It was an amazing sight to see this riot of green growth after experiencing the mostly brown scrubby landscape of the previous week's journey across the west. Truth be known, everything we had seen on this trip was nothing short of amazing.

As on the road to Pacific City, at certain points we again observed the heavy thick green moss covering trees, rocks, and draping off limbs. The best I could surmise was that the altitude played a factor in these growth zones, along with constant moisture coming in off the ocean. That was my theory, and I declared it to be a fact to Todd. He said that seemed reasonable, so it was settled.

Route 18 leveled out somewhat after crossing the Pacific Crest Mountain Range, and we came back into an area of valleys and more commercial agriculture the further east we went. The rain had stopped. In fact, it stopped once we crossed the mountains, and the sun made several feeble attempts to poke through the cloud cover but was unsuccessful in remaining out for very long. I spotted the big jet airliner sitting atop a building at the Evergreen Air Museum up ahead.

"That looked pretty weird the first time we saw it the other day, and it is still a rather strange sight today," I declared informatively, drawing Todd's attention away from his phone.

"Sure is," he answered flatly, then with more energy, said, "Hey! We are supposed to turn here!"

"Where?!"

"On the left! Right up here!" Now he was gesturing excitedly.

"We passed the museum entrance, and I do not see any road sign, so where am I supposed to go?"

"Must be by those trees here on the left. This is the address Amy sent me, and the phone says turn here!"

By now I had been braking heavily and had the turn signal on, then I saw what appeared to be a street poking out of some trees and bushes. "This is the only place I see, so I am going in!" I declared.

"I think this is it, brother!"

It looked like we were entering a small housing development, which not the kind of place one wants to drive a big RV into and have any hope of getting back out without some major problems. But it turned out it actually was the entrance to Olde Stone Village RV Park & Manufactured Home Community, which appeared to be a neighborhood of split-level and ranch-style houses. The first impression was one of total incongruity. As we crept along slowly, we arrived at a guard shack, which was unoccupied, so I drove around it at Todd's urging. Next were several signs denoting "RV Parking For Check-In."

"Well, this looks more promising!" I dryly observed. "But where the hell do we check in? One of those houses?"

"Man, I don't know! The houses up there all look the same. They are even all the same weird color blue. It looks like RV parking over there on your side," Todd observed while scanning out the windows, then noted, "That house up there has some parking spaces, and it is sort of in the direction of the 'office' sign over here."

"Call Amy! She is the one that has to go to the office and pay for this. We can just wait here and see where she goes," I said, trying to be helpful. "What time is it anyway?"

"It is 10:30 AM, which means we are way early! I think she said we can't park this thing here until noon," Todd replied, a bit surprised by the time, then added, "You call her!"

"Hello, Amy! We are sitting at the Olde Stone Village RV Park right now."

"You're early! You were not supposed to be there until noon. That was the plan," Amy replied, sounding a bit miffed.

"That was our plan too, but that did not work out so well, so we are here now," I said, trying to sound cheerful and upbeat.

Todd and I sat in the idling motor home, lost in our own thoughts. Practically speaking, the road trip part of our adventure was now over. The wholly unplanned and unexpected nature of our lives for the past week and a half vanished when we rolled into this park, and not at the scheduled time. The primary objective of the trip would soon be concluded with the delivery of the RV to its rightful owner. Plans and schedules would be imposed immediately upon our lives once Amy showed up. This was not her fault, for it is the normal way society operates, and it was going to be nice to see an old friend again. But Todd and I had embarked on this task with a mutual, unspoken sense of letting everything go, and just experience what happened. This state of mind exposed some fallacies, such as the lack of a road atlas at the start, which we corrected at the earliest opportunity. It also provided a sense of freedom, which probably was the greatest aspect of the whole journey. There were times when we scarcely knew what day it was—for it did not matter. All that did matter was that we were making progress and were thoroughly enjoying and learning from the experience.

Those factors, the learning, the enjoying, and the progress, are to a large extent what makes life itself great. From time to time we are presented with an opportunity to take the adventure of daily living to a whole new level. The lucky ones recognize it, and seize it, in spite of fears and misgivings like I had. I recognized my fears and found them to be my own baseless mental projections and facing them freed me to embrace the spontaneity of our journey. Soon the freedom of the road was going to be surrendered to the confining restraints of the normal world.

Those were my thoughts. I wondered what Todd was thinking about, but I did not want to interrupt his momentary private world, yet I had a feeling he was deep in a similar reverie as me.

Half an hour later, Amy's silver Honda did a slow roll past us and then continued on to the parking spaces in front of the office. "I think she was looking for scratches and dents," Todd remarked as we observed the performance.

"Hope she didn't expect it to be washed!"

Amy walked back to her newly arrived RV while eyeing us through the windshield. Todd leaned back to open the door, but otherwise we just sat peacefully in the remaining moment and looked back at her. Upon entering she looked at me in the driver's seat, and with astonishment declared, "You are driving?! How long has this been going on?"

"Since Lithopolis!" Todd helpfully interjected.

"I did not drive the whole way. Todd drove a lot. This has been a team effort," I stated matter-of-factly, then added, "So where do we park this sled?"

We followed Amy into the park office, which could have doubled as a doctor's office or clinic, by its Spartan businesslike appearance. It was also obvious it was a modular home, and completely different from the funky tourist campground establishments we had experienced on this trip. The park had a lot of spaces for RVs, but about half of it was comprised of the permanent factory-built houses. This was the rental community office as well as the office for transients like ourselves. With the lot assignment in hand, along with the pamphlet containing the park rules, I drove to the proper spot. Todd and I set the whole thing up in about ten minutes, all under Amy's watchful eye. She was impressed by our coordinated and professional execution of the whole process and said as much. Then she noticed a pine branch sticking out of the rolled-up awning.

"Hello, what's this?" she said while activating the awning deployment control.

"Fred had a close encounter with some pine trees!" Todd declared, smiling mischievously.

"Hey! It still has two pinecones in it! That is worth a couple of extra points for sure!" I happily declared, even though I could tell Amy did not share our cavalier attitude.

Todd set the record straight, that compared to all the things he had repaired before and during the trip, plus the new batteries he put in the smoke alarms which saved our lives on the third night, a low pine branch strike was one of the minor issues. Amy came back to earth and suggested we jump in her car for a brief tour of McMinnville, the town she was now calling home.

McMinnville, Oregon was established in the late 1800s, but evidence of those early days had been erased long ago. A good portion of the early 1900s commercial buildings were still standing, and the houses were from the 1920s on up. The town also had a newer business strip with the necessary big-box retailers. The downtown streets in the old section were narrow, bordered by several blocks of mostly two-story buildings constructed with brick, and lined by nice size hawthorn trees to create a pleasing affect. The shops were upscale clothing stores, art galleries, a lot of wine tasting places, plus a nice selection of unique restaurants. We had lunch at a decent Mexican restaurant.

Next stop on the tour was Amy's new home, which she shared with a former college friend, named Lindsay, who was away at a yoga class. The rental house was a non-descript story-and-a-half Cape Cod-style built in the 1960s, located on a short dead-end street, within walking distance of the old downtown. The adjacent houses had a bit more architectural pizazz, but not much, which made the plainness of her house even more remarkable. Interior floor space was good, especially due to the large family room, with a fireplace, which had been added to the rear of the house. Another salient feature was the reasonable rent at $1,400 per month, which seemed a bit high to someone like me, who had not rented in over thirty years. For the current economy, it was on par for renting a small size house in central Ohio, but the rent was considered low for northwest Oregon. It was the best deal they could find, and with limited incomes, there was the need to split the cost with a roommate. Brigit, Amy's Heinz-57 hound, appeared to have acclimated to her new life in town, but she probably did miss roaming the woods at her former rural home in Vinton County, Ohio.

Amy and Lindsay had a short list of things for Todd and me to move, repair, and assemble. The tasks included a floor lamp to put together, hook up the cable TV in Amy's room, final assembly of a curio cabinet, and something to do with a computer and workstation desk in Lindsay's office, which had to await her explicit instructions when she returned. We knocked out the tasks in short order, plus we found some other useful things to do and were taking a break when Lindsay appeared. She was a short pert looking woman about our age, who had suffered childhood polio but got around fairly well in spite of a painfully gimpy leg, hip, and back, which compromised some of her activity. Lindsay was also a bit intense in both her gaze and directness and possessed a keen quick intellect and a cheerful sense of humor once she opened up. We hit it off quite well once she had taken our measure. Truth is, Todd and I probably can be a bit disconcerting to someone who is not familiar with our type.

Lindsay's task for us was twofold. Move her computer to the workstation desk that had not been assembled correctly by the movers and was not in the precise location she desired. The job required tools, which she had, but was very protective of them and rationed them out only upon request. To our dismay, we were not allowed to root around in the toolbox to get what we needed. As soon as one of us set a tool down for a moment, Lindsay whisked it back to the toolbox. Unfortunately, her mild obsessive-compulsive disorder elicited a full range of razzing from Todd and me, which escalated into something just short of a whole comedy routine, much to her consternation, at first.

Lindsay ran some sort of mysterious consulting business from home, and the computer was critical. Other people had set up the current configuration, and apparently this had become an ordeal of disturbing proportions, at least for her. I asked Lindsay several times what the nature of her business was, only to receive a guarded and vague reply, but did reveal it was of a confidential nature.

I made a loud aside to Todd, "I think she is running a phone sex and live video porn operation here!"

"I think you're right!"

"I am not!" came a loud reply from the hallway.

"Well, whatever you are doing in here, this blank wall behind you cannot be improving business."

"Yeah, you need one of those tropical scene murals behind you when you are doing the video chatting, or whatever you call it," added Todd.

"I am running a business!" declared Lindsay from the hall.

"Sure, you are!" Todd and I replied in unison.

"Now I am not sure I want you guys messing with my stuff!" Lindsay stated flatly, reentering the room.

"Cool!" Todd declared while getting back up off the floor. "That means our work is done here! Got anything to drink in the fridge? It's break time!"

"Oh, come on, you guys," Amy pleaded on Lindsay's behalf.

We sized up the situation, made repairs to the work desk the best we could with disappearing tools, and moved it to the designated location – precisely. At this point, I declared the computer would have to be unhooked and reinstalled on the newly rebuilt desk. Lindsay freaked out. "Can't you move it the way it is?" she pleaded.

"Why would you want to do that? You already said it does not work right, or at least not the way you want it to. Besides, in order to get it from there to here, everything needs to be unhooked and reassembled," I firmly stated, trying to leave no room for ambiguity.

"Well, okay. But I can't watch!" Lindsay declared and turned to face away with a dejected sigh directed at Amy.

Todd and I played it for all it was worth, taking on the effect of backwoods rubes having their first encounter with technology, while yanking out wires, removing the printer, speakers, etc. and repeatedly expressing dismay at what all this stuff was used for.

"Wots this here yeller wire fer, Fred?"

"Dunno, Todd! Take it out!"

"I can do that. What 'bout this here box thingy?"

"Junk! Remove it! Hey, I need a wire to stick in a hole back here—hand me one."

"Here ya go!"

"I gots more holes back here!"

"I gots more wires! Want me to start poking them through?"

"Sure, whatever you got!"

Lindsay could not take anymore and had to leave the room. Ten minutes later the computer system had been reassembled and was up and running. We summoned her back to demonstrate. The system was functioning better than before, much to Lindsay's shock, amazement, and genuine appreciation.

Todd and I required a few things to prepare for our flight back to Ohio the next day. He needed a secure case for his pistol. I needed a backpack for the extra crap I was going to take home, like the pillow, sheet, and blanket that I had brought along, the new souvenir sweatshirt, as well as some of the food that was left over and which I did not feel right just throwing away. None of this stuff would fit in my already full suitcases. So off to Harbor Freight and Walmart we went. The necessary items were secured in short order, at which point Amy declared it was time for dinner and an AA meeting.

"Does everything have to involve eating?" Todd asked.

"I want to treat you guys for what you have done," Amy replied.

Fair enough, especially since she was not proposing to swing by the drive-thru of some fast food joint. McMinnville thrives on a lot of tourists, mostly on Saturday and Sunday, so many small businesses were closed on Monday. That was the case for the first option we selected, a Cajun restaurant, but the Italian place just down the street was open, so that is where we went for supper.

We ate at a leisurely pace—that is, Amy and I did. Todd scarfed up his meal in his typical fashion. Nevertheless, we still had almost two hours to kill before the meeting was to start, so we took a stroll down the block to the old library and the nice park surrounding it. There were several truly stunning old large pine trees by the library. The park extended down into a ravine with a small creek and continued for several blocks. Nice informative signs explained that the town got its start because of several mills that were once located in the ravine. Adjacent to the park was a street that had some fine examples of large 1910 era Craftsman-style houses, and the best architecture I had seen all day.

We approached a small group of people standing outside the building where the AA meeting was supposed to be held. There was some confusion amongst these folks regarding the meeting, such as where it was supposed to be, what time it was going to start, and if someone responsible would actually show up. There were other folks milling about wondering the same thing. Finally, some guy appeared and opened the room of the church, very late for our standards in Ohio, but sufficient to be considered on-time here. About ten people showed up for an interesting and engaging discussion meeting. Mission accomplished—got to a meeting and did not take a drink or any mood-altering substances today. That is recovery and sobriety, one day at a time.

Amy dropped us back at the RV, and Todd and I got busy packing.

Chapter 13
Separation

Tuesday, October 9-Day 10

A new day and a new beginning, only this day had a sense of urgency for we would be truly leaving the road life behind. Schedules to keep, things to do in order for the next steps to occur according to fixed plans. For all the days on the road, the plan was simply to move forward with little or no fixed agenda. Not today. We actually had places to go and things to do.

The 'getting ready routines,' comfortable in their sameness, commenced when I got up around 5 AM and went to the shower house. Being on the road, the place was new even if the routine was not. This morning ritual was to go to a shower-house which also included a laundry and a recreation room, all in one.

The sky was clear with a fine display of stars. The temperature felt like it was in the low to mid 50°s, but there was no breeze, so it was comfortable. As usual, following the shower and shave, I fixed a cup of coffee and then called Tammy. There was no answer, so I left a message. Breakfast consisted of the typical bowl of raisin bran, the last of the milk, the last of the chocolate chip cookies, and the last grapefruit. I did not want to leave anything for Amy to have to deal with later. What was left, I packed in my suitcase.

Tammy called and asked why I had not called her cellphone because she was at her jewelry class at the Columbus Cultural Arts Center. Once again, I had forgotten it was Tuesday. I figured maybe she was at an appointment with her counselor. That was scheduled for tomorrow. So much for my re-entry into the real world. I still did not know what day it was. I just knew the trip was over and I would spend tonight near the Portland airport, and I was to get on an airplane very early tomorrow morning.

Todd got busy cleaning out the RV and I pitched in. He swept the carpet and floor with a broom, and we washed all the surfaces of the mobile home—floor, walls, counters, everything. We emptied the refrigerator of all the open items and bagged up all the trash. I volunteered to take the garbage to the park refuse compactor.

Earlier in the morning, while eating breakfast, I had read the park brochure, so I knew where the compactor was, and also found out that a trail continued out of the park and over to the Evergreen Air Museum. What I had neglected to read was that a keypad combination number was required to open the trash door, to prevent non-residents from dumping garbage there. Fortunately, another resident happened by while on a similar errand and opened the door for us both. It was the same number as that required to gain entry into the shower house! I should have guessed that, but promptly forgot that number once I was in the shower.

The museum was about a quarter of a mile from the trash compactor, and a nice wide paved path ran through the adjacent 'back to nature' overgrown weed-choked field. Outside the large hanger type buildings was a fine assortment of planes ranging from a DC-9 airliner that served as Air Force Two for Presidents Reagan through President Obama, a Russian MIG-29, a US Navy F-18 fighter jet, and a Rockwell Buckeye jet trainer designed and built in Columbus, Ohio. Peering through the glass end walls of the first building I could see a lunar lander mock-up, a WWII German V-2 rocket, old bi-planes, and some racing planes from the 1920s and 1930s.

The Evergreen Air & Space Museum, just a short walk from Olde Stone Village RV Park, McMinnville, Oregon

The second building contained the gigantic Howard Hughes flying boat nicknamed 'The Spruce Goose'. This eight-engine plane, constructed with laminated wood, and designated as an H-4 Hercules cargo plane, was the largest plane in the world at the time of its only flight in 1947. Hughes built it to prove that large cargo planes were possible, and to demonstrate the strength of laminated wood and good design. No one believed that it could actually fly, but it did, with Howard Hughes at the controls, and went one mile while skimming above the surface of the water near Long Beach, California. Although the nickname would indicate otherwise, the plane was actually built primarily from birch wood. The purpose, when conceived in 1942, and when there were wartime restrictions on using metal, was to create a plane to carry troops and equipment across the U-Boat threatened waters of the Atlantic Ocean. Actual construction did not commence until 1944, by which time the German submarine threat had been virtually eliminated, but Hughes persisted in finishing the contract for one plane. With a wingspan of 320 feet, and a fuselage height from keel to the top of the cockpit of almost 40 feet, it is truly impressive. The normal-sized planes arrayed near this giant appeared downright minuscule. Being a history geek, and growing up in a family of aviators, I had been aware of the Spruce Goose since I was young. Now, to actually see it, was a genuine thrill. To have this trip end up within walking distance of this plane was just another of the many so-called coincidences, or 'luck,' that was too impossible to explain.

Todd had little interest in my aviation discoveries next door. Apparently, airplanes are not his 'thing,' and truth be known, even after a whole week together, I really could not say what if anything my travel partner was passionate about. A number of interests for sure, like politics, spirituality, and a bit of history, but possession of a deeper passion in some specific area escaped me. Maybe I should have asked. Actually, I had once while we were grinding down the Interstate but did not press the point. Todd did express a regret for not spending more time delving deeper into American history, for it did fascinate him, and his cursory understanding of many things made him an ideal travel partner for me. My interest in just about everything, with little or no filter, was mystifying for him to fathom, and he remarked about it once with amazement. It was the result of the environment I was raised in, I said, where reading *National Geographic* and studying their maps provided me with hours of enjoyment as a child.

I called Amy to let her know that Todd and I were done packing and ready to get picked up, and that the RV was ready to be hers again as well. She showed up in about fifteen minutes. We did an inspection, and showed her what was being left, like some unopened food and the big old comforter. Right beside the RV park was an RV resale business, so we went there to see what kind of deal they would do for her. It would be sold on consignment, if they could get her price, so Amy agreed to take it over to them the next day.

My next priority was to get access to a computer so I could pre-board and print out my airline boarding pass. In order to accomplish that we had to go back to Amy's house to use Lindsay's computer, if she was not using it. Ever protective of her equipment, even though I hooked it up, Lindsay balked at letting me at the keyboard for a couple of minutes. I had to show her my confirmation number and let her do it for me. I get the point, for I do not like other people on my computer, but it seemed a tad strange. Nevertheless, I was grateful Lindsay took the time to do it. Having the boarding documents in hand was a tremendous relief. The whole airport hassle, early arrival time, waiting in line, TSA screening, waiting, then waiting in line again when the boarding group is called, and then waiting in line in the airplane while attempting to get a good seat, is all a bit stressful. At least it is for me, so having one piece of the anxiety puzzle completed was a big deal, and I told Lindsay how much I truly appreciated her help, and why. She understood.

Then we were off for more running around. Todd wanted to go back to Walmart and get another suitcase. He, too, had more stuff returning home with him on the plane. It was one thing for us to just throw stuff in the RV as we embarked on this journey, it was a whole other thing figuring out how to get the stuff back while traveling on an airplane. He also had a digital cable TV converter he bought for the trip, which he wanted to return to Wally World (Walmart) because he did not use it. Amy and I leaned against the car and talked, enjoying the warm sun in the parking lot, while Todd took care of business.

Next, it was back to the old downtown of McMinnville. Amy had a hair appointment. She was getting shaggy and really needed a trim. Actually, Amy has her hair cut short, and she had not had time to get this done since she arrived in town, plus she did not know who to trust with the job, so it kept getting put off. These are the small things that add up when one makes a move to a new community. Where is the closest drugstore? Are any doctors accepting new patients, and will they accept whatever insurance you have, or just as important, does your medical insurance recognize any of the health providers in the new area? Just some of the things that she was slowly taking care of. Today, it was hair.

Day 10 *Two views of downtown McMinnville, Oregon, our final destination.*

Todd and I declined the option of sitting around while the stylistic negotiations took place, so we went out for a walk around downtown. First, we strolled down to the railroad station where I took some pictures. Then we walked back up the business block while looking in store windows, and we killed some time in an antique store. Todd also goofed around a life-size bronze statue of Benjamin Franklin sitting by a bank. What the correlation was, we could not figure out, but it was a fine rendering of this inventor, philosopher, and one of the founders of our country. By now we were getting bored, and if things continued in this vein we would probably start to get in trouble with the natives, so we thought it best we go hang out on one of the sidewalk benches near the hair emporium, and try to behave ourselves. That was a tall order. Snarky comments ensued about passersby, or the occupants in the vehicles cruising by, or the vehicles themselves, much to our own amusement. Though somewhat inappropriate, it was liberating to know that we would probably never be back to this place, and never see these people again, nor would they see us. We were not being loud or confrontational, and if anyone had noticed us they would probably assume we were merely two older guys having a good time—which was exactly the case. Figuring it might be better if I put my time toward a more constructive activity, and because our boisterous nature might result in us being asked to leave the sidewalk bench, I got up and dialed Tammy on my trusty flip-phone. Leaning against a building where I could keep an eye on the entrance to Amy's new hair establishment, I gave Tammy an update on our slow progress toward getting to the airport. As we were talking, I spotted Amy exiting the building.

"Amy wound up with a new hairstyle! She looks rather 'butch' and she is not going to like it!" I narrated to Tammy as Amy waited to cross the street. We concluded the call, for I was not sure what would be next on the schedule.

Sure enough, Amy was not pleased. "I don't think that woman listened to a word I said about how I wanted it! I am not happy! But what can you do?"

"I think you look darling!" Todd declared with an extravagant wave and a mischievous smile.

"Maybe after a couple more sessions you can get her trained properly," I offered in consolation.

"It will take four months for my hair to grow back! By then she will have forgotten who I am!" Amy replied in protest. Then, changing the subject, Amy looked at Todd and me, and asked, "So what have you guys been doing while I was in there getting scalped?"

We eyed each other sheepishly. Todd cheerfully declared, "Nothing!"

"Oh, no! I know you too well to believe that!"

"Well," I replied hesitantly, "There was a slight incident with Ben Franklin."

"What did you guys do?!" Amy asked excitedly. "That is my bank! I have to show my face in there! Am I going to hear stories about two guys and the statue the next time I go in there?"

"We did not tell anybody that we knew you!" Todd declared, with exaggerated innocence.

"Good grief! Can't leave you two alone for a minute!" Amy replied, shaking her head in bewilderment, then declared, "I'm hungry! I will buy you lunch. if you behave!"

"Yes, Mom!" Todd cooed while giving Amy a hug. "I really like your hair!"

"Shut up!"

We headed up the sidewalk and entered a large storefront that had formerly been the local department store, but now traded in a plethora of artisanal goods. There were racks of women's fashion items interspersed with displays of strange handy-crafts, decorations, and potions in exotic containers.

"I thought you were going to buy us lunch! These handbags do not look edible!" Todd loudly protested.

"Would you behave?!" Amy hissed sternly. "I was told there was a nice place to eat in here."

"Maybe it is up there on the mezzanine," I said while gesturing toward the upper rear level of the big main sales floor.

"What's a mezzanine?" Todd loudly asked, in his best hillbilly accent.

"It's a balcony," I replied.

"Well, why didn't you say so?" Todd protested, then putting his arm around Amy's shoulder, innocently added, "He's using big words again, Mom! He has been doing it all week!"

Todd and I were both laughing now. Amy swiveled away from Todd and headed toward the stairway. The small dining area at the top of the stairs contained about a dozen tables and most were occupied by fashionably hip looking folks of all ages. They appeared to have just come out of an Abercrombie & Fitch, or L. L. Bean catalog. We looked positively thrift store in comparison, which was entirely true in my case. A small table by a window was available, so we claimed it.

The restaurant was called Sage, and a bit more upscale from the 'greasy spoons' I normally frequent, however, the prices on the menu were quite reasonable, especially for the savory fare being offered. Todd had an interesting exchange with the young pretty waitress regarding the difference between a lentil and a dried bean, which left Amy shaking her head, but the waitress was mildly amused and a good sport about it. Lunch was very tasty and leisurely. We talked about Amy's future in her new town, and things about our shared past. Of any place to make a new start, this one was as good as any, and better than most, so we wished Amy well.

The hour and a half drive to the Portland airport was mostly uneventful, except for the dueling mapping systems Amy and Todd opened on their phones. Amy's insisted on staying on the I-5 right through downtown, even though she knew of a better route using the by-pass. Todd's directions tended to agree with Amy. A lack of clear street signage made finding the way to the Ramada Inn rather interesting, especially with the phones telling her to turn where there did not appear to be a road, yet the Ramada was in plain sight. Amy found a back way into it, somehow.

Todd and I checked into separate rooms. Although we were both leaving early in the morning on different flights, it seemed less stressful if we took care of ourselves from this point. We were so busy trying to navigate our ways through the maze of hallways that we really did not have time to wish each other well for the next part of the journey—our trip home. Later, as evening approached, I texted Todd a message of appreciation for our fine adventure and hoped he had a good flight home. His message back was a similar heartfelt expression of appreciation.

It was a sudden and bittersweet end. Todd and I had been in close proximity to each other for ten days. A bond of trust and friendship had been forged by travel, driving, working, eating, and lots of conversation. It could have been so much different, and not in a good way. Now, here we were, instantly on our own, yet strengthened by our shared experience and personal growth. I had an overpowering sense of peace and serenity, yet wistful to have this engaging odyssey abruptly conclude.

Chapter 14
Homeward Bound

Wednesday, October 10-Day 11

A wake-up call from the front desk of the Ramada Inn at PDX was scheduled for 3:45 AM. Several times during the night I woke up to glance at the digital clock radio, afraid I might miss it. Around 2:40 AM I decided 'the heck with this' and got up. That gave me ample time to shave, shower, and get a cup of coffee without being rushed before heading out the door. Tammy called as I was getting dressed to make sure I had gotten up. The front desk rang the phone two rings for the wake-up call. I was glad I was already up because I would have slept right through that wimpy effort.

The Ramada Inn Airport Shuttle was to pick up passengers at 4:20 AM, so I loaded up my stuff and headed for the lobby. The clerks somehow knew my room number as I crossed the shiny marble floor, so I tossed the room keycard on the desk, thanked them, and went out the door to the van. There were two other early flight passengers already on board.

Portland International Airport (PDX) turned out to be rather impressive in size and in architectural design. Its modern flowing glass wall front façade rose several stories high above a multi-lane passenger drop-off ramp. A massive sweeping glass canopy covered a walkway connecting the terminal to a huge eight to ten level parking garage that had vines growing on it, which reminded me of the Hanging Gardens of Babylon, though I could not be certain that was the intended reaction.

The Transportation Safety Administration (TSA) security screening seemed to be a bit more of a hassle than normal. Even at this early hour, the lines were full, and the airport anxiety level was palpable. Not all airports require removal of shoes anymore, but this one did, and although I had my driver's license ready, they also wanted me to remove my wallet from my pocket so the TSA agent could rifle through that as well.

He was less than amused when I remarked, "As you can see, I am broke!" so he demanded that I empty my pockets. Out came three paper napkins and a rock I picked up from the beach at Pacific City.

The humorless man cleared me with a curt, "move on!" With the smug knowledge that my pocket contained yet another rock, I hauled the trays holding my possessions over to an area of benches where I put my belt and shoes back on and reloaded my pockets.

Southwest Airlines Flight #150 from PDX to Chicago Midway was sold out, so the waiting area was packed. I felt good in the knowledge that I had an "A – Group" boarding pass, which meant getting on the plane in the first group, so a window seat should be all but assured. Then the gate attendant started calling special groups for pre-boarding. Military personnel, people with disabilities, people with special needs, then families with small children. Those of us already lined up as Group A began to shuffle around nervously. It appeared that half the plane would be filled before our esteemed high group ranking would be acknowledged and we would be permitted to trudge down the flyway. One family had five or six small children, several of whom were ensconced in strollers that looked like small covered wagons. One little boy in this large clan was having a complete meltdown that included screaming, stomping his feet, going limp, running away, and punching his mother in the face several times after he was apprehended, all while she was holding a young infant in a chest sling. Nobody could board until this drama played itself out. Finally, the shrieking child was corralled, and the family with their convoy of wheeled equipment was sent trundling down the passageway. More than one stunned witness shook their head in amazement while muttering, "Whoa, this is going to be a very long flight!"

Upon boarding the plane, it was hard to determine where the ballistic child was due to the confusion of loading overhead luggage bins and the whine of the idling jet engines, so I grabbed a window seat by the wing. Luckily, the family had been banished to the rear of the plane, and with the exception of a couple piercing screams, I never heard or saw them again.

The plane lifted off through a light drizzle, then rose above a low layer of scattered puffy clouds. It was still dark, so the lights of the Portland suburbs were clearly visible below. As the climb continued, we went through another layer of clouds and burst into the dawn.

As it turned out, the whole country was covered with this layer of cloud cover. The only exception was Yellowstone Lake and the snow-covered mountains just to its west. I thought I recognized the shape of the lake, with its small island to the south, from studying our map when we drove the park less than a week ago. Judging by the snow now on the ground, I was glad we were not attempting that trip today. In actuality, the park was probably closed for the season now.

Day 11 *Passenger departure drop off zone, busy at 5 AM, Portland PDX airport.*

Glow of sunrise. Southwest flight 150 PDX to Chicago

A break in the cloud cover reveals snow covered Rocky Mountains, and what I presumed to be Yellowstone Lake.

I found some diversion taking a few pictures of sunrise reflecting on the plane wing and of Yellowstone Lake, otherwise, the unending flat cloud cover made for a boring flight. A young woman in the seat next to me occupied her time on her laptop computer, switching between attempts to work on a spreadsheet and a lame movie. I tried reading a *TIME* magazine I brought along, but mostly I nodded off a lot. She and I did talk briefly as the plane approached Chicago. She asked if I was a professional photographer, due to my large film camera. She was heading home for a visit to some town I probably never heard of called Parkersburg, West Virginia.

"No, I have heard of it. In fact, I go by Parkersburg quite a lot because my folks live in Marietta!"

"Oh! Well then you probably know where Williamstown is! That is actually my home."

"Yes indeed! We have eaten at DaVinci's many times. That is a good place. My father recently passed, so it is just my mom now, and she actually lives in Devola. I imagine you know where that is since you are from Williamstown."

"That's amazing! One of my best friends lived in Devola!"

"It is a small world! I assume you are on the next flight to Columbus from Chicago."

"Sure am!"

"Well, if I do not see you on the next flight, have a safe trip, and enjoy your time home."

She smiled, nodded, and replied, "You, too!"

There was an hour layover at Chicago Midway Airport, which gave me time to eat a very expensive blueberry muffin and drag my stuff over to another concourse for my connecting flight, Southwest #2220 to Columbus. I gave Tammy a call to let her know I had arrived back in the Midwest and should be home in a couple of hours. It started raining hard. I took a few photos of the ground crew getting soaked while servicing a plane.

Servicing a Southwest plane in the rain at Chicago Midway Airport.

Planes lined up on the taxiway at Midway.

The trip home, via airlines, was the absolute opposite of the way we had traveled out west in the RV, which was less stressful due to the lack of any schedule. Fast is good, but the slow way is even better.

As I walked off the plane in Columbus, my phone rang. It was Tammy, and she was in the 'cellphone lot' over by a MacDonald's restaurant west of the terminal. I told her to wait at least ten or fifteen minutes before swinging around through the "Arrivals" pick-up ramp because it would take at least that long for me to get my luggage and haul it out to the sidewalk.

Outside at last and having a much-desired smoke in the designated area at the pick-up zone, my phone rang again. Tammy was lost. Well, technically she was not exactly lost for she knew where she was, and it was not where she was supposed to be. She had asked a cashier at MacDonald's the best way to get back to the terminal and was given some rather sketchy directions. Tammy found herself going down Sawyer Road, which she knew was wrong, and ended up on Hamilton Road a mile east of the terminal. Having the presence of mind to get turned around, she was heading back in a mixed mental state of panic and being irate. I assured her it was fine, and I would put the extra wait to good use by burning up another cigarette.

Watching the comings and goings of cars and people, while keeping an eye out for Tammy's white Hyundai Genesis Coupe, I spotted my seatmate from the PDX to MID flight stepping off the curb. She glanced to the right and saw me, and we gave each other a wave.

Tammy arrived. She was exhausted and in a foul mood and wanted only to be out of the driver's seat and heading for home. There was no kiss, and she backed away from me when I tried to give her a hug. I was not entirely surprised. She had been pissed when

I left, pissed while I was away, and still pissed now that I had returned. It bothered and disappointed me, but I had just concluded a memorable experience and I was not going to allow the dark demeanor of my spouse to become a total buzzkill for me.

One thing Tammy does rarely without fail is fall asleep in a moving vehicle. The silence during the drive home was not awkward—just the opposite actually. It was almost peaceful in spite of the cloud of gloom hanging over my unconscious partner in the car. She awoke as we got off US-33 and on to North High Street in Canal Winchester.

"I'm hungry!" she declared. I was too.

We opted for Shade on the Canal, a sports bar type of establishment in what used to be a rather renowned family restaurant in the 1960s and earlier. It was an easy choice since we were driving right past it. While waiting for our salad and pizza, we talked a bit about the trip, not just to be civil, but because we care about each other. It was proof to Tammy that I had not forsaken her. I had not died while off on what appeared to be a fool's errand, especially one that had turned into *Pee Wee's Big Adventure*. Her anxiety, frustration, and anger of the past week and a half slowly began to release its strangle-hold grip.

Before the main course arrived, I received a text from Todd. He was at the airport waiting to get picked up.

"Are you home yet?"

"Close but needed food. We are at Shade's"

"Cool. Just wanted to know if you needed a ride!"

"Thanks, brother! Have a good evening."

Tammy went to bed as soon as we got home. She was fried and exhausted from the stress of the day, and of the whole trip. It had been a long day for me as well but I took the time to unpack because I was still too stressed from the day's journey. Everything went into the laundry basket, to "clean up the wreckage of the past," as it were. My clothes still smelled of RV exhaust and burnt plastic even though most of them had been washed back in Wyoming. Go figure!

I tried to go to sleep but could not. I was too wired, and my body was now on Pacific Time, which was three hours earlier than home in Lithopolis. Sleep finally arrived around midnight.

The long adventure was over—well, not quite over. The next day I felt like I had a hangover. I assumed this bad feeling to be "jet lag" and it was the first time I had ever experienced this phenomenon to this extent. Chalk up another first for the books.

Chapter 15
Aftermath – Renewed Faith

Tammy had her own journey while I was away on mine. The nature of the phone calls was a product of her own fears, plus having to deal with issues on her own, such as the coughing up blood scare which surfaced her fear of cancer. Thankfully, that turned out to not be the case, but she still had to face it alone. There were other things as well, but that is her story to tell.

Two days after my return home, Tammy wrote in her journal and shared her thoughts with me. It shows her growth. It also illustrates the strength and foundation of our relationship and provides a fine coda to this story. Here it is, in her own words. (Some words omitted, and some punctuation added for clarity. Used with permission.)

12-fri-Oct '18

   3 AM- I'm Up. I feel good! I feel myself — wipe that smile off your face, son(!) — ha! . . . well, see, I guess I even showed myself just (how) much I love & adore Fred. I guess I have to admit that this stupid trip of his has opened the door on / to a whole new perspective of him, me, & us. Apart we can (& have) functioned just fine, & together we operate like a well-oiled machine that loves being together. And I guess that Higher Power that makes things "GO!" knew exactly what it was doing, for it showed Fred he could still function as one, (and) manage to find his way around a map & a good time independently, while back at the Ranch it (my Higher Power) showed me I could still live life, take care of business, & handle crisis, alone & independently. Yet we both know ultimately our place is together in our home. So, all was / is good.

  Thank you, God

Epilogue

I am grateful for having taken the chance on a truly once-in-a-lifetime opportunity and experience. It turned out far better than I could have imagined. Todd was a great traveling companion—both as a friend and as a skilled fixer of disasters.

The whole trip was blessed by God, and that I truly believe. Who I traveled with, where we found ourselves on the journey, and which roads we took, reached far beyond the mere fortuitous. Nothing besides the destination had been planned. Everything else was just made up as we went, and at the end of each day, we felt as if there had been some guiding hand in it all. It was an exhilarating feeling. It was also like being in a meditative state, while moving.

The fact that Todd and I have similar spiritual beliefs and background, as a result of our shared journey in recovery through Alcoholics Anonymous, made it relatively easy to let go of the normal constraints of life, especially once we were on the road. The process of "Letting Go," and turning the result over to a Higher Power, allowed us to truly 'be in the moment' each minute, and each mile, for days upon days. Once acquired, that is a sensation that does not depart. It is spiritual in nature. I can still feel it now and am thankful for it.

Maybe this sort of thing happens to all those who go out on what morphs into an adventure. Maybe that is why they do it. But I believe the spiritual connectedness only happens to the lucky ones! We are all blessed with the ability, for God has granted us that gift. Those who are aware, and embrace that gift, become truly conscious in the moment, and each succeeding moment. For the others who set out on travels, the result is probably in the satisfaction of having accomplished something, even if it is just checking off another item from a list. I hope the list checkers eventually stop and wonder about the deeper revelations possible during their journeys. In that regard, I am truly blessed, for I was conscious of a deeper significance the moment the wheels started rolling. Prior to that, my consciousness was bound and restrained by fear and anxiety.

During and after, Todd and I talked about such things. We agreed it felt like a 'guiding hand' was with us. It was not just me; it was both of us. The fast car in the night that led us out of Yellowstone, and then vanished. Finding places to stay when all the usual suspects were closed for the season—a season that we were only vaguely aware of. Snow closures just hours after we had passed through. The list is infinite—so is the sense of appreciation and thankfulness.

I wrote things down in a journal while we were traveling. Todd joked to Amy that I was writing a book. Tammy said that maybe I should write a book, because something definitely happened to me, and she wanted to know what it was. Try as I may, I do not feel like I can really do it justice. It is a deeper feeling, a deeper comfort, which my words struggle to describe.

The evidence will have to be in my being—my actions, thoughts, words, and deeds on a daily basis. Everything else is not in my control.

    The world is large, fascinating, and stunning. This trip barely scratched the surface of our great land, and it was a wondrous sight to behold and experience. Few can take a trip such as this, and it is not necessary. Make the next trip to the corner store, the post office, or just out the back door, your own memorable journey!

Thanks to all who made this possible—before, during, and after!

Fred Rutter
Lithopolis, Ohio
Sunday , January 27, 2019

References

Alcoholics Anonymous World Services, Inc. *Alcoholics Anonymous.* (*also known as the "Big Book"*), New York, New York. first printing 1939, fourth revised edition 2001

Alcoholics Anonymous World Services, Inc. *Twelve Steps and Twelve Traditions.* "Tradition Eleven: *Our public relations policy is based on attraction rather than promotion; we need always to maintain personal anonymity at the level of press, radio, and films."* pg. 180, New York. April 1953

Dolnick, Edward. *Down The Great Unknown: John Wesley Powell's 1869 Journey of Discovery and Tragedy Through the Grand Canyon.* HarperCollins, New York. 2001

Google Maps. website, www.google.com/maps

Scott Lothes, "Gliding Through the Cascades," *Trains Magazine,* (November 2018), p. 34-43

Yellowstone National Park. website, www.nps.gov/yell

Thomas Moran, artist. website, www.Thomas-Moran.org/biography

Howard Hughes, Spruce Goose. website, www.evergreenmuseum.org/the-spruce-goose

Rand McNally. *Road Atlas 2018*, Chicago, Illinois. 2017

Wyoming Department of Transportation. *Official State Highway Map of Wyoming*, Cheyenne, Wyoming 82009. 2018

Eisenhower Archives, "The 1919 Transcontinental Motor Convoy".website, www.eisenhower.archives.gov/research/online_documents/1919_convoy.html

Wallis, Michael. Williamson, Michael S. *The Lincoln Highway: Coast to Coast from Times Square to the Golden Gate*. W. W. Norton & Company, New York. 2007

Cody, Wyoming. WyoHistory.org A Project of the Wyoming State Historical Society. Lynn Johnson Houze 2014. website, www.wyohistory.org/encyclopedia/cody-wyoming

Wikipedia, Mount Rushmore. website, www.wikipedia.org/wiki/Mount_Rushmore

Musson M.D., Robert A. *Catch Route 22! A Pictorial History of U.S. Route 22 and The William Penn Highway*. Zepp Publications, Medina, Ohio 2015

Acknowledgments

Alcoholics Anonymous (AA World Services, Inc.)
PO Box 459 Grand Central Station
New York, New York 10163
212.870.3400
www.aa.org
contact your local AA Intergroup

National Alliance of Mental Illness (NAMI)
3803 North Fairfax Drive Suite 100
Arlington, Virginia 22203
703.524.7600
www.nami.org
Help Line   800.950.6264

Badlands National Park
PO Box 6
Interior, South Dakota 57750 – 0006
605.433.5361
www.nps.gov/badl

Badlands Interior Campground & Motel
900 SD HWY 377
Interior, South Dakota 57750
605.433.5335
www.badlandsinteriorcampground.com
www.badlandsmotelcampground@gmail.com

Mount Rushmore National Park
13000 Highway 244
Keystone, South Dakota 57751
605.574.2523

Black Hills National Forest
Black Hills & Badlands Tourism Association
605.355.3700

Whispering Winds Cottages & Campsites
12720 South Highway 16
Rapid City, South Dakota 57702
605.574.9533
mail@whisperingwindsblackhills.com

Ponderosa Campgrounds
1815 8th Street
Cody, Wyoming 82414
307.587.9203
info@codyponderosa.com

Yellowstone National Park (National Park Service – U.S. Department of the Interior)
PO Box 168
Yellowstone National Park, Wyoming 82190-0168
307.344.7381
www.nps.gov/yell/index.htm

Stinker Truck Stop #45 / Roady's Black Canyon
I-84 Exit 13   5220 Black Canyon Road
Caldwell, Idaho 83607
208.454.9179
www.stinker.com

Cape Kiwanda RV Resort & Marketplace
33305 Cape Kiwanda Drive PO Box 129
Pacific City, Oregon 97135
503.965.6230
info@ckrvr.com
www.capekiwandarvresort.com

Olde Stone Village / RV & Manufactured Home Community
4155 NE Three Mile Lane
McMinnville, Oregon 97128
877.472.4315
www.oldestonevillage.com

Evergreen Aviation & Space Museum
500 Northeast Captain Michael King Smith Way
(off Oregon State Route 18)
McMinnville, Oregon 97128
503.434.4180
www.evergreenmuseum.org

Google Maps
www.google.com/maps

Rand McNally. *Road Atlas 2018*, Chicago, Illinois. 2017

The Photo Place, Inc. *film processing – developing / printing / image digitization*
480 South Canfield Niles Road
Youngstown, Ohio 44515
330.799.7771
info@photoplaceonline.com

Gorham Printing Company   *formatting, layout design guidance*
3718 Mahoney Drive
Centralia, Washington 98531
800.837.0970
www.gorhamprinting.com

Special Acknowledgments

My mom & dad, Betty & Joseph Rutter, for their lifelong encouragement, and tolerating me through the years when I was lost and did not know it, and especially my mom for encouraging me to keep on writing.

Tammy, my wife and partner for 27 years. We have gone through some tough times, and for Tammy, this was certainly one of them—and then I started writing this, which partly kept the wound from healing. We are also best friends and traveling buddies, and she is always ready for the call of, "Road Trip!" no matter how near or far. I Love You.

Dear friends Tom & Amy Karshner, and Todd Brady, who made the trip possible. You will be forever in my heart and memories. (Tom, you would have loved this trip, and would have been proud of Todd and me. You were with us in spirit, all the way.)

Joe Todd & Linda Fraker, friends, and fellow travelers, who provided worthy input, criticism, and encouragement during the initial stages of this project.

To all the great people we met along the journey. This story would not be the same without you. Same goes for all the great places in this land, and the roads that connect them.

About the Author

Fred Rutter has been sober for decades, and actively pursues a life of recovery and spirituality on a daily basis. He has lived in central Ohio his whole life, and resides in a small rural town in a very old and funky house along with his wife and a number of cats. This has served as a convenient location to travel the country extensively. Writing and photography have both been hobbies since adolescence.

He attended Wilmington College in Wilmington, Ohio, plus Ohio Northern University and Columbus State. His job experience is as varied as his education, and has worked in warehouses, sales, a factory, construction, bartended, and driven trucks. He eventually gained stability through sobriety, and retired following a 27 year career at Mid-Ohio Foodbank, primarily in transportation, logistics, and management. Mid-Ohio Foodbank distributes food to over 650 hunger relief agency partners across a 20 county area of central and eastern Ohio.

Mindful living and spirituality are important aspects in his life, which is enhanced by travel, writing, photography, and collecting old paving bricks.

He uses a Minolta X-700 35mm camera body, a variety of lenses, and Kodak film (because that is all that is available now)

Photo credit: Tammy Rutter 2020
Moonville Tunnel, Vinton County, Ohio